CW01629663

EMOTIONALLY CELTIC

This book is written by a Celtic supporter for Celtic supporters, and you will find yourself in here. After all, we all did the same things. Being a Celtic fan is an identity you should be proud of. No one can take that away from you. Hopefully you will laugh and cry through the following pages.

Matt.

EMOTIONALLY CELTIC

Matt McGlone

GD COMMUNICATIONS

First published 1995
by G.D. Communications Limited
60 Wilson Place
Nerston
East Kilbride
G74 4QD

**British Library Cataloguing-in-Publication Data.
A catalogue record for this book is available from the British Library.**

ISBN 0 9527156 0 0

Cover designed, printed and bound in Great Britain by
Garthland Print Ltd., Glasgow G51 2RL

The above photograph was taken in 1967.

Dedicated with much love to my Father and Mother.

You do something to me
- something deep inside

I'm hanging on the wire
- for a love I'll never find

You do something wonderful
- then chase it all away

Mixing my emotions
- that throws me back again

Acknowledgments

This book is dedicated to my Mother, Father, and my three children - Kirsty, Gary and Nicholas.

I would also like to thank four men whose calibre I won't encounter again. Colin Duncan, John Thompson, David Cunningham and Brendan Sweeney.

The book is all about Celtic Football Club and the many ways it can affect our lives. Our formative years are our most important. It is when our love for the club is ingrained on our minds. We carry this forever. When you love something in life you must protect it. That is all we did.

I would like to thank the following people who made it possible for me to write this book. If they didn't contribute materially, then they contributed spiritually: Jock Stein, Jim 'Flax' Flaherty, Joseph Gaughan, Tommy Burns, Cathy Ryan, Fergal O'Kane, Fergus McCann, Bruce Welch, Stephen 'Carrots' McGhee, Arthur Haggerty, Michael Anthony McEleney, Davie Higgins, Jim Cameron, Tony Ford, Nicky Stewart, Jim Stevenson, Margaret McGinley, The Kirkshaw Kangaroos, Fabrizio Ravanelli and Allessandro Del Piero, and finally Mark Graham and Paul Keenan along with the rest of that gang.

For their help with production: Kevin McKenna, David Low, Gerry McWilliams, Martin McWilliams, Allan Cowan, Des Browne, John Paul Eadie. To Ian and all down at Garthland Print for doing a wonderful job. Thanks for all your help and patience.

Thanks to ... Tony Murray, 'The Evening Times', 'Scotland on Sunday' and 'The Celtic View' for their kind assistance with the photographs.

My apologies if I have missed anyone out.

Many women have played a part in my life as Celtic were tied to me like an umbilical cord. Thanks for your help and what you put up with. If we lost out through it, I'm sorry. It wasn't me who was in control.

To Celtic supporters world wide, who care about what they love and believe in. It's yours, look after it.

Contents

Growing up a Young Celt

I came to the conclusion early in my youth that supporting Celtic was more than just cheering on your team every weekend. We are involved in something which, whether you want to believe or care to admit it, has a grip on your mentality, and will shape part of your life. Unless you divorce it totally by not going at all, then you are under the spell that binds us to Celtic.

So where do you reckon all this started, and do you think you had a choice in the matter? I would reckon you probably didn't. Many people say it is a form of tribalism, and that's where I think you do have a choice.

Let's say that you are 14 or so and you want to go to the game with a bunch of mates, all of you will either wear a scarf, a team jersey or another item of Celtic clothing, the reason being that you want to be identified as a Celtic supporter. All the same, people may say that because you are always in a large crowd when travelling to the match, then you could be described as being in a tribe. Therefore, you chose your method of how you attended the game.

There are quite a few other groups a fan may be described

as fitting into. There are too many to mention, but to show a comparison, you wouldn't be described as being in a tribe if you travelled alone, went with a couple of pals or took your son or daughter to the match.

So if people want to label it tribalism, then fine, as long as it is not violent, then tribalism won't do anyone any harm at all. If you want to be seen to belong to a group, then it is only something that has been going on since time began. I have followed Celtic in a tribe and I have followed Celtic outwith a tribe. But here's the rub. When we are all singing and dancing together on the terracing we are a tribe and make no mistake about it! There will probably never be another occasion in your life when you will turn around and hold a stranger close to your body, grab his hand, and maybe end up kissing him as well, is there? Let's face it we have all done it, as the ball bulges in the net! Right, we have now identified that we belong to something, in this case, it's the Celtic. You are now identified as being a supporter of Glasgow Celtic. Now, whether you like it or not, you are now also part of the sectarian divide. If a Rangers fan decides he wants to insult you, he may well call you a 'Fenian B'. This will be done, perhaps because you are wearing an item of clothing that is simply Green and White. He has identified you!

Now whether you are a Protestant or Catholic Celtic supporter, you will still fall into this category. Your opponent in the Blue corner will assume. He won't be verifying your religion before he delivers his greetings. Therefore you belong to one side of the sectarian divide.

If I cast my mind back to when I discovered that I, just like you, were cast on the side of Green and White, then I'm sure it was before my first day at school. But that is the first time I can actually recall it.

On my first day at school I walked out of the front door at number 25 Drumoyne Circus with my head clothed in a balaclava. On the way to St Constantine's RC School myself and a pal walked down through Drumoyne Road into Nimmo Drive and eventually into Uist Street. Now in those days, March 1960, 'boys were men'. We went to School ourselves, none of this getting your mammy to hold your hand all the way.

I had never been in this part of Govan before, and I really didn't take much notice of the school across the road, which was called Elderpark Street. Playtime arrived, and as we milled about in the yard a rock or a brick landed at my feet. "Where did that come from?" was my immediate thought, with my head shrinking into my body, half expecting another to follow.

It, of course, came from our Protestant brothers across the road. I have forgotten hundreds of things in my life, but not this. This incident has always stuck out in my mind, and at this precise point in my life, I understood very clearly, the 'us and them' bit.

Don't get me wrong, the stone-throwing wasn't all going in one direction. It was two-way traffic, and who knows who threw the first stone? Now, before we go any further, let's look a bit closer at this introduction. Was it healthy? Definitely not. So why was it happening? This, I think, is important. It was happening because, before we even attended a football game we were divided as children. Now Celtic and Rangers play a part in all of this, but not at this stage.

This happened because two branches of the Christian Church broke asunder around 300 years ago over several points of doctrine that each held dear. It is at this point we were divided. My children go to a Catholic School because myself and their mother went to a Catholic School, and that is the way we want them educated.

In my time at St Constantine's we sang to the same tune as the children across the road, but with different words. For us it was 'Proddie dogs eat the frogs, two for tuppence ha'penny' and they retorted with 'Catholic rats eat the cats, two for tuppence ha'penny'. Now this was all one upmanship, because if they sang at you, then you sang your song back, and vice versa. When you think about it, it is the very same at a Celtic and Rangers game today, except, of course, the tunes and the words have grown somewhat in sophistication.

Is all of this bad for the mind? I mean would we have turned out any different if we had been brought up, say, in a rural farming area, or on an island which only had one school?

Who would sing or throw stones at you then?

My conclusion is this. That is simply the way it was and as you grow older you begin to work it all out. Your mind sort of accepts it. If you have no friends on the other side of the fence (whichever side), then don't be too surprised if people refer to you as a bigot. We all have friends who are of the other religion. It can only be healthy and, therefore, we have learned and come on a bit since that first day at school. So if it got to you that bad at five, and you haven't been able to shake it off, then I think it was bad for the mind, and that's sad.

Put it this way, if you have taken the religious thing that bad, then you will have missed out on the 25 glorious trophies Jock Stein brought to our Club and you will not have recognised or appreciated the fantastic contribution people like Kenny Dalglish, Danny McGrain, Davie Provan and many others have made to the Celtic cause.

You may have missed out on your ideal partner in life. You may also have missed out on having some very good friends. It is definitely not healthy and I am sure that the vast majority of Celtic supporters are above all of that.

Celtic and their traditions mean everything to me. The reason they were started, the culture they created, the important principles in life which are part of us all. The identity they have created within us, this is all part of our life. It has formed us into the very people we have become today. If your principles are carefully nurtured and you can look at life in an open manner, then you have got it made.

There is nothing wrong with loving what you love in a big way, if it is inoffensive. If what you love is the Celtic, and others take offence, then the problem is not yours, it's their's.

Perhaps, you would not be wrong to suggest that by supporting Celtic, you probably have a chemical imbalance in your brain. I mean, explain the trigger that went off inside your head when as a child you listened to a Celtic victory on the radio, or even better when you were at the game.

The first thing you probably did was rush into the house and have a mad search for your ball. In my case it was a World Cup, or a Wembley ball, (remember those big heavy orange balls?) Nothing else mattered - clothes were thrown all over the place, and members of your family were brushed aside during this manic wee period.

And then you found it. You had it in your hand, marching out the door with your chest stuck out like big Billy McNeill's. Nobody could defeat you.

You would immediately think of who's door to chap. Some would be fellow Celts. For me I always wanted to chap the door of a Rangers fan, especially if they had been beaten that day; there was a certain glowing glee about your wee body when they answered the door.

You didn't even have to say anything. That look on your face told him. "Hi Rab, fancy a game of football? Five half time, eleven the game." If he could stomach your agitated state, he may well have come out, and made sure a couple of those John Greig tackles were good late ones. But if he was sickened sufficiently by your presence on his doorstep, then his answer would be along the lines of "Naw, I canny. Ma maw says ma tea's ready".

Even if it took another half an hour, you would still get your team together. Your mates, half mates and others would somehow appear, and you could stop touring the streets with your ba' under your arm. The initial verve you had when you first searched an hour ago for the bit of plastic was still there, and it would remain there until you scored, shooting the ball past the jumpers and jackets for a glorious hit.

Jinking past a pal, you would pretend to weave your hips just for pure cheek, and if he was really duff you would spin back and beat him again. Everybody wants the ball and you find about eight people around you at once. "Here, here, come on, here, here." No, they are not looking for a cat, they are wanting you to pass the ball to them. Then you would end up losing it, and being called all the greedy B's of the day.

But that magic wee moment wasn't far away and one you could experience everyday. You have scored, and you turn away thinking you are a Celtic player. In your head the fans are going mental and cheering your name. You turn and spin all at once, a quick glance at one of your mates and you shout

"Johnstone, one-nil" or "Wallace nine-eight."

Your mum had no chance of getting you into the house, even when she tried to entice you by taking out a roll and chips which ended up being your dinner. You would play until it was dark, a streetlight would quickly become a Celtic Park floodlight, and you were the player on that stage. One day I would be Jimmy Johnstone, the next I would be Bobby Lennox. If I felt like being cheeky I would be Bertie Auld. If I hit a rocket shot from way out, I was Tommy Gemmell. In defence heading it away, I was Billy McNeill, and nobody was going to tell me any different.

These were magic moments in our childhood and the marvellous thing is they all happened in our heads and nobody can ever take them away from us. It's as if they are locked away in a wee private vault. I look at my two sons today and they do exactly the same thing up in the field near their house.

Today it's Van Hooijdonk and Thom, they imagine they are. And as I watch them turn away, taking the imaginary acclaim from the crowd, I have a wee chuckle to myself and realise they too are locking away their private dreams.

Although kids don't play as much in the street these days, I don't think the jumpers and jackets down for goal posts will ever disappear.

These small stadiums we all played on will always be there. One will go and another will replace it. I played on a bit of grass which was a sort of triangular shape, and it was also on a bit of a hill. This was on Crookston Road, right at the bottom of Kempsthorn Road, in Pollok.

Immediately across the road we had another wee pitch. This one didn't have floodlights though, as the streetlights were too far away. This particular stadium was just off Crookston Road, adjacent to Leverndale Hospital and measured about 15 x 20 yards. Sadly, there are houses built on it now. Each time I drive past it I can recollect the odd golden goal, and wee Jimmy comes flashing back. Do you think those kids who live there now realise the history they have in their back garden?

We had moved to Pollok from Drumoyne in 1962. 'We' being my father, mother, my sister Mary and me of course. I was 8 and Mary 11. All it represented for me was a change of scenery, different mates, a different school and a room for myself.

Mary went to the fee-paying Notre Dame School in Glasgow's Hillhead, and would shortly be sitting exams to progress to the secondary version. She was a very studious girl, and I was the total opposite. Even though I was only 8 years old and probably couldn't spell Notre Dame, age wouldn't have made any difference anyway, because I was more interested in outdoor pursuits than sitting in studying. In life it's horses for courses. My course was never for studying. On the other hand Mary's course was all for studying.

All of her hard work has now paid off and she is happily married, to a Vice-President of the Motorola Corporation. They've got three children and are living in Austin, Texas. Mary's daughter Catriona has just enrolled on an four year course, studying Pre-Med and Medical Ethics at The University of Notre Dame in Indiana. This will be followed by a further four years at medical school. So if you see me wearing a Notre Dame baseball cap you know where it came from!

When Mary went to Notre Dame it was a bit of a daily trek for her. A No.23 bus from Crookston Road, outside the big wall at Leverndale Hospital. From there it was onto Govan Cross, and a subway over to Hillhead. I remember one day when she came home from school, she was telling my dad that there was this man, with a creepy beard, called Pastor Jack Glass in and around Byres Road.

I don't think he ever said anything direct to the Notre Dame girls, but they were taught exclusively by nuns, and the fact that he was in evidence occasionally, as well as his reputation for making anti-papist slurs, was perhaps enough to make the Notre Dame girls that wee bit apprehensive.

My Dad explained what this obnoxious wee man was all about, and from what I gathered through the years he became more of a joke than a threat. I always remembered him as a sort of Scottish version of Ian Paisley.

At this point in my life I was more interested in making new pals than anything remotely academic. We lived at 3 Beltrees Crescent, right on the corner, with a big garden. Across in Kempsthorn Road lived the Cavanaghs, and I became friendly with the two eldest brothers, Peter and Andy. Now, here's a funny thing. Mr Cavanagh came home from work one night and had pens with football teams' names printed on them. We obviously all wanted the Celtic ones, but he didn't have enough Celtic pens to go round and Peter volunteered to take the one marked Rangers. Although we probably made a smart wee comment at the time, Peter, in fact, began to support Rangers because of this incident, and although I haven't seen him since 1972, I know he has preferred Rangers since, and it was all because of this pen, given at an early age.

In 1963 the Bhoys were not doing too well. They did make it to the Scottish Cup final though, and played Rangers before a crowd of 129,527. With a Bobby Murdoch goal the game ended 1-1. Eleven days later the Bhoys lost 3-0 in the replay.

In those days the League Cup was played without a sponsor and the teams qualified from sections. Celtic were paired alongside Dundee, Dundee United and Hearts. Unfortunately they never qualified from this group.

Players around those days included men like Frank Haffey in goal. I'll stop right there at Frank, because even although Frank lost nine goals playing for Scotland at Wembley he lived less than a mile from me, right at the top of Crookston Road, in Mulben Crescent, and was most definitely a local hero for me and the other wee Tims around our bit.

You've got to remember that Celtic players were regarded as being something supernatural to us. I thought that you could never emulate these people because, well, they played for Celtic and they must be sort of special. You know they were made with an ingredient that you didn't have. We were in total awe of this guy because he did something that we could only dream about, and he lived just up the road. I must have lost count of the amount of autographs I got from big Frank, half of them were on bits of paper we would pick up in the street or on old fag boxes.

We would go up and stare at his windows until he came

out, only the bold chapped the door. "Imagine we were his paper boys, can you imagine it?" "Oh I couldnae deliver his papers, ah mean how do you ask him for the money?" These were the kind of things we would say to each other as we stood outside staring at his curtains.

I remember vividly once when Frank came out with a bucket of water to wash his car. We all charged into his drive at once. "Eh Frank, can I have your autograph?" "Hey can you write on this?" It was right at this point where you got that wee buzz inside you. Here was this icon and you had captured his attention for the amount of time it took him to sign the autograph. I think possibly, that is where you experienced the buzz from, because you had his attention. Yes definitely, you had him captured. "Do this for me big man, and make it snappy." As if we would be so bold to even think this. I mean he might notice it on your face or something and he wouldn't be your mate any more.

As we pushed around his car the water splashed over Frank's shoes and trousers. Mad panic attack coming up. "Sorry Frank, it wisnae me." "Watch it stupid, look what you've done to Frank's shoes." Big Frank shrugged it off and said he would have to go and get his dinner.

"Hey Frank will we wash your car for you then?" I think the slight demented look on Frank's face told us it was time to walk back down Crookston Road. As a small postscript to Frank: Once we had lost that big awe we had of him, we would regularly go into his back garden and raid his apple tree. You know those big cookers that gave you a sore stomach after you ate two or more!

Because of these escapades with Frank, I remember I would stick up for him in his absence when people said he was duff. This would continue until I was about 11 years old. Frank by then had gone to live in Australia, so I replaced him with other heroes.

Enter the Lisbon Lions, but that's in another chapter. The last I heard of big Frank was that he had been playing down under and was entertaining the fans by walking on the crossbar with his hands prior to the game starting. At the end of this season in 1963 the incomparable Jimmy Johnstone was forcing himself into the first team. He made his debut against Kilmarnock at Rugby Park on March 27. Celtic lost 0-6. "Maybe this wee guy with the curly red hair isn't that good after all!" Other players from that time were Paddy Crerand, who received the 'Once A Tim Always A Tim' fanzine at his Manchester home each month until it ceased in 1994. In fact Pat was the very first person I interviewed for the fanzine in December 1990. Billy McNeill was there, so was Stevie Chalmers, as was Mick Jackson whom I have met a few times in the last year or so, an absolute gentleman I may add. Bobby Lennox was breaking through, as Willie Fernie went in the other direction, and Charlie Gallagher, a big favourite of mine, and a vastly underrated player in his day.

It's strange how people's paths cross where Celtic are concerned. After the Boardroom takeover in March 1994, myself and the four other 'Celts For Change' members were invited by Fergus McCann to be special guests of the Club when Celtic played against Motherwell at the tail end of season 1993/94.

Prior to going to Celtic Park that afternoon I decided to nip into St Enoch's Square in Glasgow to pick up a few items. I jumped a taxi near my home in Shawlands. As you sometimes do, if the driver is sociable, you end up having a wee chat. After a few minutes the silver-haired driver, who had his back to me, said: "Are you not Matt McGlone?" "Yes," I replied. Now let's hold it right there, because this man has turned around, and no matter how much the years may have changed him, I know it is Charlie Gallagher. Now when I see Charlie Gallagher, I see one of my etched-in-the-brain Celtic memories, which comes flooding back into my head. I am 12 years old again and my dad has stood in a queue a week or two earlier for over 3 hours to get both of us a match ticket. This is something I probably didn't even appreciate then. I mean he was buying me a piece of Celtic history and I probably didn't even say "Thanks Dad". If only I could return the compliment to him now. But I know I can't, and will never be able to, and that upsets me as I type out this part of the book.

His actions in standing in that queue, had enabled him and I to stand in amongst the 75,000 fans for the 2nd leg

Quarter-Final European Cup tie against Vojvodina Nova Sad, from Yugoslavia.

Celtic had lost the first leg 0-1 two weeks earlier and the Slavs who had dismissed Atletico Madrid in the previous round were well fancied to put us out. During these memory flashbacks, distinctive parts of the day always stick out in your mind. This particular day was bloody freezing and I was despatched to Parkhead bound in my balaclava.

On big nights like this, as I was small, my Dad always took me to the Rangers End. Although the entire stadium was packed with Celtic fans, he always reckoned that there was maybe just that little bit more there room to move around. I reckon he was right. At the previous European night against Nantes we had waited until the crowd had almost gone. Near to where we were standing, my Dad noticed a home made step which a child would stand on to make him that wee bit taller in a big crowd.

It was obvious that whoever had left it had gone by now, so I carried it off home, looking forward to using it in the next tie, and I did, against Vojvodina.

Celtic were one up with a minute to go, and needed a second. We won a corner at the Rangers end at the stand side, just where we were standing, with me on my box with my balaclava keeping my lugs warm! "Dad, Dad, do you think we'll score, will we, will we?" He gripped my hand tightly, and said "Son, this is it!"

I stared down at the floodlit pitch open-mouthed. Charlie must have been blessed, because he flighted over a corner which I swear on my kid's lives hung in the air for big Billy to rise like a Pheonix from the ashes and his header totally bulged the back of the net. Mayhem had arrived at Celtic Park and my wee world went mental. I was tossed around like a cork in the sea and I loved every minute of it. By this time my balaclava was all over my face!

Times like this made my world. Total strangers kissed and hugged each other. Remember that I had been to all of the preceding European nights that season, therefore I was used to strangers hugging and throwing me around. This was a magic I wish my own children could experience. It's a vital part, I think, of being a Celtic fan.

So here I am 27 years later, sitting in the back of a guy's Taxi, on one of the biggest days of my Celtic life, when Celtic are about to honour me and four diehards for our efforts in saving the Club from going into liquidation, and the guy complimenting me for my efforts is the guy who helped me store my eternal memories. And I am expected to cope with this. I was blown away, and to make it all worse, Charlie didn't even take the fare. Day's like this can never be planned. But I will point out one factor in all of this which made everything possible. My love, your love, our love. The Celtic.

Glasgow the Divided City

As I was relatively new to Pollok, I was still in the process of making new friends. I had secured a paper round and living right across the road from us were the Garrett family, Billy Garrett to be precise. Now the Garretts had a dog which they loved dearly. They were what you would call a pretty Orange family, and they had somehow trained their dog to go for Catholics. When they shouted the word 'Catholic', the dog went berserk. I remember at this point I was the paperboy and I really didn't want the Garretts' dog to eat me!

So I have a dilemma. Do I just stop delivering their paper or do I attempt to work it out? I decided on the latter, it sort of went like this: "Hey Mr Garrett, you know how you said your dog is trained to bite Catholics?"

"Aye that's right"

"Well I'm your paper boy, what about me?"

"Aye it's OK, it knows you." And believe it or not, I actually understood what he meant, even at that age.

It was like, because the dog knew me, and even although Garrett might shout 'Catholic' it would ignore him because it had seen me around. I'll tell you this: any time I was passing a butchers shop I would make sure I got old Billy Boy a bone! It was best to keep on his right side than cut about Pollok with a high pitched voice!

Now as a boy of 12 I knew exactly what sectarianism was, although I had probably never heard of the word sectarian. It stood out a mile, you know. You are walking down the road and you know that the older guy coming in your direction might just kick you in the balls. For one reason, and one reason only, because you were a Catholic. The strange thing was you knew this, and if he did toe you, then it wasn't exactly a shock.

April 12th, 1967. A drizzly sort of night. Although your younger days can be sketchy, certain things stick out in our lives. Some of these memories will come flooding back when somebody mentions something, and suddenly you will have a recall. It may be in five minutes, it may be in five years, but you will experience a recall, and it will take you by surprise. When it comes keep it close to you. After all it's all you've got.

For this particular memory I need no such prompting, as I have carried it with me since the day it was formed in my head. My dad parked the Ford Corsair miles down London Road. In those days thieving wasn't so rife, compared to now. I reckon that if you display a radio today, then unfortunately you may expect to have your window smashed on your return.

Back to my memory, and I will cherish it forever. Me and my dad are walking up London Road towards Parkhead. He's taking my hand and I'm staring at the floodlights, dying for a macaroon bar! The floodlights have always held some sort of fascination. Even today I can't explain the magic they held, they just did. A feeling enveloped me, a sort of, 'I'm safe, I'm excited, I'm going to the game, and those floodlights are getting bigger by the yard!'

Just walking up that road, being part of those evenings was something, and although I remember it well, I don't think I appreciated the enormity of what it meant. Here was me all made up. "I'm going to the game with my Dad. I'm part of the show, the action. All of these people going in this direction are going to the same place as me."

Because Celtic were so good, you had this self-assured, sort of smugness about you, without ever having to display it. This is where Celtic really get etched into your brain. This is formative. This is your education, and all I'm thinking of is macaroon bars!

The game itself, was, as expected, another glory night. It was very easy, remember, to take all of this for granted. The previous Saturday we had beaten Motherwell 2-0 at Fir Park. I wasn't there because my dad was a hairdresser and we only went to home games and only when it was dry.

But this victory had taken us to within two points of the title and it was only April. Willie Wallace with a rocket shot, and big Tam Gemmell with a penalty, and the show was over. Dukla Prague though, according to my dad, would be a harder team to beat; all of their players were in the Czech Army. I suppose that made them sound sort of tough. You know, a Czech Army team, big muscly guys all with the same haircut and faces that never smiled, and they would look dead mean. But we had big Jock, and Jock could work out everyone, and any problems they may present. He gave you that assurance.

In the previous round against Vojvodina, Celtic had worn their all-green strip. What a cracker! This time they were back in the magical hoops. Dukla were a clever team and had one brilliant player in their side. Although he was getting on a bit he was very special. His name, Josef Masopust. This guy had played in the World Cup Final against Brazil in Chile five years earlier. Dukla were no mugs. They had just dumped Ajax who had themselves put out Bill Shankly's Liverpool 7-3 on aggregate in the previous round. Celtic though, were quite happy with the draw, because they had avoided the favourites, Inter Milan who in turn were paired against the Bulgarian Champions, CSK Sofia, in the other semi.

From memory, Celtic romped forward at electric pace, and the first goal came not long into the game. Wee Jinky killed the ball with his chest and lifted the ball over their keeper. 1-0, and there goes another balaclava! Almost right on half-time they scored. "Wait a minute, Dad, this isn't in the script." He was useless at this point, because he said nothing.

All of my feelings now rested on big Jock, because he had a magic wand and he would be bawling and shouting at the players in the dressing-room, wouldn't he? And somehow he could retrieve this situation, because he would tell his players what to do and it would work, wouldn't it? Well that's what I thought anyway.

Strangely enough over the half-time period my Dad never spoke much. This made me suspicious, because he always told me that we would sort them out and things would end up fine. Perhaps he was losing his bottle, and I would have to reassure him that things would work out fine in the end.

I needed reassurance at this point. That was his job, wasn't it? I needed to be told that we were going to score six, and where is he? Lost in his own concerns, and I'm getting fidgety.

I generally reckon that the team who lose a goal just before half-time are perhaps a little more down than the team who have just scored. But Celtic came out like men possessed and 14 minutes into the second half they scored. Tommy Gemmell punted the ball from defence, Willie Wallace chased it relentlessly and stabbed it into the back of the net with his right foot. There goes that balaclava!

Just six minutes later, and me still adjusting my balaclava, like a woman applying make-up, and we score a third. A hand ball gives us a free kick. Bertie Auld who, by the way, has a growth like Desperate Dan, hovers over the ball like a wily old fox. As the army boys tried to build a preventive wall, the Bold Bertie slips it to Wallace lurking to his right.

Their keeper Victor never moved a muscle. Wallace crashed it home and this time my balaclava was taking residence in New York! "Yes, yes, yes!" I'm jumping all over the place. I'm holding people I've never met. People are screaming. Some are kissing each other. It's bedlam! But where's my Dad? I want him to tell me what I already know, and that three goals are enough, and we can't lose in whatever country this team come from. There he is, his car coat is almost over his head, he's hugging me now. This is great, wait till I tell my mates at school. They'll be wishing they were here.

I always used to think when I was at these great European

nights, that going back to playing normal league games was a bit boring. We seemed to be on another planet, with Rangers and the rest of the teams mere easy beats, and totally boring. I remember thinking as we walked out of the ground with the floodlights lighting up London Road, almost all the way down to Bridgeton Cross, that I only had seven more days to wait to get excited Celtic style again. That was a Scottish Cup dress rehearsal against Aberdeen in the league. It ended up 0-0 and we were one point away from the title.

Ten days to go and we would be playing Aberdeen in the Scottish Cup Final. The team which played that day, April 29th, is the very same team who ran out 26 days later against Inter, and Willie Wallace who had scored two against Dukla Prague, obliged with another two. One in each half, in front of a stunning 126,102 crowd at Hampden.

All this hugging and happiness I'm having at the football makes it sound like me and my Dad are like big mates. Well that was not quite the case because he was strict and liked to instil discipline, and to be honest, he never really budged much from that stance until many years later.

He had a hairdressing business in Skipness Drive, in Linthouse. I had no choice in the matter and was made to work in his shop on a Saturday with loads of women around. Some would be nice to you because they knew you were Frank's son. That was probably the worst thing about it, because he would enforce this really dead serious, no fun atmosphere around me. I, on the other hand wanted a bit of a laugh. But to achieve that you either had to make sure he wasn't on the scene, or wait until he had got near the end of the day, when he would relax a bit, and then I could make an appointment with him to have a laugh!

As far as haircuts were concerned, I had the standard crew cut. Not because I wanted it, but because he said I was to have it and that was that.

Football at this time depended on two things. One: how busy the shop would be. Two: the weather. I now know why my mother would constantly say: "See that boy he keeps looking at the weather. Come away from that window!"

Now we are talking about any window here and not just my Dad's shop window. I was almost addicted to looking out the car window, looking out my room window, looking out the window at school, pulling up the venetian blinds all over the house. You know those ones that cut your hand when you had to clean them.

I kid you not, I could tell you the names of all the different type of clouds. I could just about predict, as I watched the clouds getting thicker, and thicker, working out almost to the half-hour, when it was going to rain. I'm not talking about showers. I'm talking about real serious heavy rain! Friday night, after the news, on came the weather. I wouldn't allow anyone to turn the telly over.

The reason for my obsession was because my father would tell me that we would go to the game only if it was dry. Now, that's torture isn't it? How can you settle down and concentrate on all those heads you had to scrub when you were looking out of the bloody window every five minutes!

My tasks in 'Frank McGlone's' were to sweep up all the dead hair, empty the bins, go the messages, smile at the right time, put on the tea , help old 90-year-olds on with their coats, open and shut doors for the customers, and, of course, look out of the window. But I was not allowed to answer the phone, because I had not received the required amount of elocution lessons at that stage of my head scrubbing apprenticeship.

My real apprenticeship was in 'expert massaging' of the scalp. Well, that's what they would tell you it's called in Chelsea, but down in Govan I knew it as 'another heed to wash'.

On a normal Saturday I could wash 36 skulls, no problem. I got quite good at this. "Bend your head over a little bit more please, that's great." Then it would be "The water's not too hot is it?", when really all the time I'm thinking of the match, and the only way I would know I was roasting their scalp was if my hands were burning! I can tell you this: these customers were lucky I wasn't wearing rubber gloves. If I had been, there would be a few baldy woman cutting about Govan today. Come to think of it, there are plenty anyway!

One day there was a classic incident. I'm 13 years old remember, and this big fat woman with a 100 inch cleavage has water flowing down her front, because I'm not holding the hose properly (I was most likely staring out of the window at the time, you know, at the clouds!). It starts to drip onto the floor, and I'm thinking that she is, like, doing the toilet.

I discovered later that the reason she didn't want to say anything, was because she knew what the old man was like. She had witnessed me getting a 'thick ear' in the past!

I'm hosing away and she suddenly looks up and says "Hey son, you're no holding that hose right, watch your Faither disnae see ye."

I just grabbed a big lump of cotton wool that was used for doing the perms, and just about stuffed it down her humungous cleavage in a mad fit of panic! The cotton wool was made like rope to suit the perm curlers, but by now it looked more like an umbilical cord hanging from her! 'He' meanwhile is oblivious to all of this, as he has his back to me, cutting away.

Close call!

Tips were not really handed out in my direction. It was usually the stylist or the junior who benefited financially. There were occasions though, and there's one I won't forget in a hurry. A customer gave me a shilling as I helped her on with her coat. My father was standing close by and was observing my manners as I said thanks in triplicate. "Buy yourself some sweets, Matthew."

Now, if someone gave you money when you were young, I'm sure you bought what you wanted. After all we are only talking five pence, which is a bit different from having a fiver to spend. Anyway, I nipped into the newsagent next door and bought myself, believe it or not, a 'Celtic View'.

I didn't see a problem here, but the old man did. "You were told to buy sweets with that money."

The customer was still in the back shop and was about to come to my rescue. "It's okay Frank, it was just a suggestion."

Things went a bit quiet until the customer left the shop,

but I knew exactly what was coming, I mean there was no way he was going to lose face over this. "Take the paper back to the shop, and buy what the customer told you to buy." To save myself getting a 'thick ear', that is exactly what I did. I was 13 years old and it is something I have never forgotten. This was all to do with a parent dealing with a teenager, with him determined not to lose face, and to show me he was still boss, although not for long.

Earlier I had been told that I was going to St Aloysius' fee-paying Secondary School, and not to Lourdes Senior Secondary in Cardonald where all my mates at St Monica's were heading. The reason behind this thinking was because my sister Mary, the Academic, went to the private, fee-paying Notre Dame in Hillhead and was being taught by Nuns.

I was so opposed to this, it was unreal. I couldn't imagine walking around Kempsthorn Road with a St Aloysius' blazer on, while all my mates went to Lourdes. You can imagine the scenario. They would all be standing at the bus stop and they would have on the college-type jumpers we wore in those days: the Ben Sherman button-down shirts, hipster trousers, Gloverall duffel coats, and Frank Wright Terry shoes with around 35 segs in each one. And then there would be me in the grey flannels, green blazer, with what looked like a Golden Eagle on the left breast, and the accompanying wording underneath: 'Ad Majora Natus Sum.' And last, but not least, a cap. You might well have just yelled out: "I am a Fairy!"

I would have found it difficult to have survived this considering the district I lived in, and no matter how well you got on with your pals, a division would have been created. And I would have stuck out like a sore thumb at that bus stop. "Check him. Look at his posh blazer!"

Why should I have been ridiculed like this, with no retaliation possible. How could I possibly defend myself physically and fight for my pride, which was everything at that age, when I have that blazer on my back. No way. I had made my mind up. I wasn't bloody going. Parents who want to send their kids to these schools should be able to afford taxis there and back as well as the fees!

I have always held the belief that if your heart is not in

something then there is no point in getting involved, no matter what it is. You are better keeping your energy for something you appreciate better. How can you give your all, when the outcome of your efforts is going to be something you hate?

I am not making excuses in advance here. This is just the way it happened at the time. I had an entrance exam to sit. Now you may as well have given me a key to release me from this nightmare scenario, and put me on that bus to Lourdes with my mates.

It would have been around about Spring 1967: Celtic going for the European Cup and me supposedly going to St Aloysius'. From memory it was a bright and sunny day, I know because I spent half the day looking out of the window. There was the exam laid out in front of me. Right Matt, if you go for this full pelt you may pass, then again you may not. Who will ever know? What did happen (in between looking out of the window) was me putting pen to paper in no particular rush. I also remember it was difficult, therefore I would have needed a fair bit of time to get through the papers. Unfortunately (ha, ha!) I didn't get accepted, and the papers weren't completed, so who knows how I might have done?

So with that wee episode behind me, it was onto Lourdes, in Cardonald. This was a two-bus journey. One from Crookston Road, down to outside Safeway's in Paisley Road West and another, usually a No.54, going to Cadder, but dropping us Pollok boys three stops along the road opposite the Moss Heights flats.

According to true life, myth and legend, Lourdes was the first school in Glasgow to have floodlights. Apparently, the decision to install lights was taken after a vote amongst all concerned, and it was either floodlights or a swimming pool. All the girls, of course, voted for the floodlights, didn't they, and that was that!

At Lourdes we would have almost 50 to a class, from four different areas. Also, at this particular time, gangs came from every area. Sometimes you would have two gangs from one area. Lourdes had pupils from Pollok and the gang representation from that district were the 'Pollok Crew' and the 'Bundy'.

From Penilee we had the 'Young Pen'. From Govan we had the feared 'Govan Team' who also had members who lived in Pollok. The two that I knew of were Babbs and Baldy. Babbs was a guy called Peter Babbington who lived in Kempsthorn Road, just up the road from where we lived. The 'Govan Team' were becoming spread out in quite a few areas of Glasgow's south side, mainly because many parts of Govan were being bulldozed.

Paint-spraying was a big thing and the 'Govan Team' had a particular design with three letters 'GTR', which would be sprayed over the top of each other, a bit like the badge on the Rangers jersey. This meant 'Govan Team Rule'. Each gang would have a short saying, but would only use the first letter of each word. For instance 'TYB' meant 'Tongs Ya Bass!' That really meant 'Watch out!'

We had a garage right next to the house. One morning my father was running us to school, and as he went to open the garage door the logo 'GTR' was sprayed on it. I had a sort of nice, funny wee feeling about this. Don't ask me why, I still can't figure it out today. I knew immediately it was most likely Babbs who had paid us an overnight visit. Any time Peter was walking by he would always give me an "Alright, wee man". He was a Celtic supporter and I remember him telling me years earlier that Celtic Park was called Paradise. "Is it Babbs? How do you know that?"

The old man was furious and was shouting "Who did this?"

He looked at me while I'm trying not to laugh. "Do you know anything about this?"

"Naw, it's terrible, intit? I don't know anyone who would do this."

"I'm going to find out about this" he said angrily.

"Aye, so you are" I thought to myself, "You've nae chance. I'll know who did it before you even come back from your work."

Another gang represented at school were the 'Car-d', funnily enough from Cardonald. They were probably the least feared and did more spray-painting than sword-fighting.

Back at school I remember in the library on the first day, one teacher taking the names of everyone who would from now on be in this new class. "Name?" "Kennedy." "Name?" "Docherty." "Name?" "Hanlon." "Name?" "McGlone." "Spell it." "M, small c, G-L-O-N-E." "You there, Name?" "Howe, Sir." "How, because I'm asking you. Name?" "Howe, Stevie Howe, Sir!"

Now for a moment or two I'm thinking we have a real star on our hands, a guy on the first day at school giving the teacher the complete run-around. But that wasn't the case and Stevie was one really good guy whom I got on well with.

There were always boys at school who were really good at football, and Stevie Howe was one lad whom I was sure was going to play professional football. He didn't for some reason, but he certainly played a lot of junior football and was a well-thought-of player at Pollok Juniors.

I remember watching Stevie limbering up in the 1980s at Hampden in the Junior Cup Final. Through injury he ended up as substitute that day, and I recall thinking that this would be a big day for him and that it was a shame he wasn't getting on from the start.

At Lourdes we had a teacher called Matt Lynch who played for Celtic in the 1930s and 40s. Andy Lynch, Tommy Craig and Tommy Coyne were former pupils, the latter coming after my time at school. Me? Well, much as I tried I was never going to get a game for the school team. That's how good I was!

Christmas day 1967, and after Mary and I had cleverly removed the chair from the other side of the living room door, (this was the McGlone parents' security measures, to keep us from getting to the presents in the middle of the night!) I found an envelope with my name on it. By this time father had made his presence known in the living room. "Before you open that Matthew, if you can tell me what's inside, I will give you five pounds."

Now, I'm looking at my mum with those pleading eyes, like "Do you know, and will you tell me what is inside this envelope?"

That was met with a 'you'll-get-me-into-trouble' look. A

fiver was no inconsiderable sum then. I hadn't a clue and got no help from any quarter. I'll just have to rip it open then, which I did.

Inside were two tickets for the New Year game against Rangers at Celtic Park on January 2nd. I looked forward to the next seven days with real excitement. Waking up on the morning of a game against Rangers was a great feeling and I doubt if that feeling inside me has changed at all since.

Nowadays I may get up early, sit around and read the papers, make a few phone calls, and very little else.

That day we drew 2-2 with goals from Murdoch and Auld.

I was playing occasionally for Cardonald Boys Club. We played down at the 50 pitches at Moss Road, Shieldhall. The club was run by a guy called Mr Cathcart. I don't think he liked me very much. Don't know why. It just seemed that way. One day my dad noticed an advert in the 'Evening Citizen', which read "Celtic Boys Club. Players wanted. Phone the following number."

I applied and got a reply telling me to turn up at some hall in Maryhill I think. This was for training and I reckon anyone looking about at all the excited faces would know that we were all trialists. After training with them for about four weeks, I eventually got my trial. All of us trialists had to play the existing Celtic Boys Club team of that age. The game was to be played on Glasgow Green, and we all ran along the street to the Green after changing in the nearby St Luke's School hall, on Ballater Street, in the Gorbals.

I'm afraid that this turned out to be a total nightmare for me. Looking back, I suppose the entire evening was a mistake. The reason being that my father, mother and big sister, Mary all turned up to cheer me on. I was trying to please obviously, and kept looking over at them to see if they were watching me. As far as the game was concerned, it passed me by. I got whacked a couple of times and contributed just about nothing.

At the end of the trial we all ran along Ballater Street back to the school to get changed. As far as I was concerned I knew my fate, unless they were looking for a ball-boy. Once we got changed we were all to stand in a line. Jim Torbett was running the Boys Club at this time but from memory I don't think he delivered the bad news.

Anyway, whoever it was came along the line and broke the bad news to 10 of us, the words of which still ring in my head today. "Sorry, you haven't been accepted." I think just hearing that, although it came as no surprise, was sort of hard to take, and I remember some of the boys who were much better than me, getting a bit upset.

Teenage Rebellion

This year, 1968, was the year for rebellion. I was 14.

Now my Father, although very strict, was a good man. I think I began to work him out about then. I mean how long was I going to walk around accepting 'thick ears'.

Celtic, meantime, had won the League again. They also won the League Cup, beating Dundee 5-3 in the Final. On the way to the final, Celtic had been scoring freely and had beaten Rangers 3-1, Aberdeen 5-1, Ayr United 6-2 and Morton 7-1. This type of form hadn't been evident in the Scottish Cup and we lost 2-0 to Dunfermline at Celtic Park.

We also went down 2-1 at home in the European Cup and drew 1-1 away to the Russian champions, Dinamo Kiev. I was at the home tie, and that evening a young reserve called George Connelly walked around the entire pitch playing keepy-uppy with the ball. I watched in amazement as he did a circuit of the park without dropping the ball once.

As I said, it was the year for rebellion. My Dad had taken a heart attack and suffered a stroke. He had been in hospital for some months, but thankfully recovered sufficiently to leave hospital, but he had lost the power of his left hand and his hairdressing days were over. For a man who had worked all his life, to be suddenly put out of work was a cruel psychological blow and through time I noticed his tight rein on me beginning to relax.

When he came out of hospital my hair had grown somewhat, and although I was a regular visitor to the hospital, he didn't seem to notice the fact that my hair was approaching my shoulders. I will always remember this conversation and where it took place, and the importance it had on me. We were sitting at the kitchen table, and it was a Friday. I knew something was coming, because the air was quite tense.

He asked "What's with the long hair?"

I replied "How do you mean?"

"Your hair, it's long."

"I know, I'm growing it."

"What are you growing it for?"

"Because I want to!"

Now as far as I was concerned this was the breaking point. If he had said, "cut it", I was prepared to defy him and say no, and I had never said no to him before. As always a saving grace can appear from out of nowhere, as we both tried to stare each other down. Mothers being wise people, can spot this stand-off situation quite early.

"Frank, it looks okay. He's not going to grow it that long anyway. Are you?"

"No, I don't think so." And the situation had been defused. I think all young boys at that age have experienced this type of situation, whether it's over a haircut or whatever. There will always be a shifting of sands between the father and son.

Times and attitudes have changed and my twin sons who are 14 years old, dress and do what they want with their hair and have always done so. I don't blame my old man's strict attitude. Remember he was brought up in the 1920s. It's just the way he was, but I also had to progress at the same time.

As if by fate another showdown appeared, and again it was at the kitchen table. He had stopped going to the games, and was beginning to wonder who I went with, and, more importantly, what part of the ground I went to. Now, if you have just escaped from your father's clutches, and are now an adolescent, you are hardly going to go into the front stand and shout "Come on boys play up the game!" or "Oh that wasn't a very nice tackle, Referee!"

I was right into the 'Jungle' with a 'tricolour' draped on my back, cape style, like Batman, and the Celtic scarf around my neck, or sometimes it would be around my wrist. I loved the community singing; this was my identity, this was my second home.

We were beating everybody then. Rangers were a joke, and I was learning to sing all the songs. Being in the 'Jungle' at this time was magic. The atmosphere made you feel ten feet tall and everybody was your best mate.

This was raw Glasgow emotion and what a buzz I experienced from it. Replica strips weren't available, but most youths of my age wore hand-knitted v-neck jumpers or cardigans. I had a green and yellow cardigan with patch type pockets, and a pair of neatly-creased Wrangler jeans. This was match-day uniform, although I usually had to sneak out of the house wearing something else over the top, as I wouldn't have been allowed out like this.

The 'Jungle' was a university and you would learn a lot about life in there. To be streetwise was as good as having a couple of highers at the time. This could also be said to be true, even today.

So at the table my Dad is quizzing me about my whereabouts, and who I am hanging about with.

"How do you get to the game?"

"I get a No.23 up to Midland Street, then I get a No.64 to Parkhead under the big bridge at Argyle Street."

"Whereabouts in the ground do you stand?"

Now, I must admit, I hesitated here. I had to risk him throwing a flakey if I told him the truth in those precious seconds. I decided not to risk it. "I go to various parts of the ground, it depends."

"Depends on what?"

"You know, it depends on how busy it is."

I reckon I had got away with as much deflection of the truth that I was going to. He then leaned right over in my direction and, for a split second, I thought perhaps one of those 'thick ears' was about to make a comeback!

"Look, don't you come in here with any of that 'Jungle' talk, right!"

Stuttering slightly, I said "What do you mean?"

"Don't give me that, and don't try and be smart, you know what I mean."

At the start of the following season 1968/69 we played Clyde away from home, winning 3-0 with goals from Lennox, Gemmell and a relatively new face, Jim Brogan, who had played about 18 games the previous season and was now beginning to become a regular member of the first team.

Our next match is one I won't forget in a hurry. It was against Rangers at Celtic Park on September 14.

Rangers won 4-2 so I'll be brief about the match! Willie Wallace scored our two. London Road at the time had tenements down the right-hand side, which proved to be lucky for me. Going down London Road, the Celtic fans would walk down the right hand side, and Rangers fans down the left. The police usually had it under control, but occasionally there would be charges from one side or the other, and hand-to-hand combat could ensue. Put it this way: if they got hold of a Celtic fan and he was on the deck there wouldn't be anyone in the Rangers crowd to help him out. The boots would go flying in and you knew the score.

My experience of Rangers crowds coming out of a match was that their mood would be the same towards anybody in green and white. Whether they won or lost, it was, well, a green rag to a bull. You would be in real danger even if you just happened to be passing and you were wearing some item of clothing that was green.

This particular day they had just won 4-2, and the usual insults were flying back and forth. As we neared Bridgeton

Cross a large group of them charged towards us. It was run or get your head kicked in, and maybe worse.

The cops by this time were nowhere to be seen, and as we were hopelessly outnumbered, it was every man for himself. I became separated from the rest and ended up running up a close. I can remember all the yelling quite clearly. "Get into the Fenian B's" and "Kill the B's."

I'm flying up these stairs five at a time, banging on doors on the way to the top. Not one door opened. At this point I reckon I have just completed the Rosary! I'm out of breath and my heart is pumping. As I reached the top I heard the noise of more people rushing up the stairs. My immediate thought was, stuff the scarf up my jumper, and walk down the stairs very casually, as if I lived there and I'm going out for a wee walk. This was the only way I could think of surviving a major kicking, Glasgow style.

As I walked down, casually whistling some pop song, I was ready to take on a look of total surprise at the on rushing Rangers fans, as I was sure I was about to get done in. But no, my prayers must have been answered, because the guys rushing up the stairs were four other Celtic fans. They looked at me with as much surprise as I looked at them. I quickly pulled out my scarf to identify myself ,and we all took a deep breath. Luckily, no one else came up the stairs.

Even now, when I'm taking my sons, who are season-ticket holders, to a match I try to talk them out of wearing colours to the Old Firm games. It just isn't worth it. Having experienced the savagery that goes on after these games, the last thing I want to think about is my lads getting set upon just because of the colour of clothes they are wearing. That's what sectarianism does to people. Support your team and your beliefs to the hilt, but don't get involved in nonsense at football games.

Not long after I started to go on a supporters bus which left from outside Donnelly's Bar in Govan Road. There was always more than one bus which left from outside pubs. Donnelly's was situated in between Govan Shipbuilders and the Lyceum Cinema on the other side of the road.

December 1970 and time to enter the big wide world.

The House of Fraser had advertised for a Trainee Window-dresser and I applied, thinking I was reasonably good at art, and ended up getting the job. I worked in one of their many stores, Muirheads, in Sauchiehall Street. It's long gone now, but Boots the Chemist stands on exactly the same site.

You know what first days are like. Your head's in space most of the time, as you desperately try to look like an adult. The last thing you want anyone to say is "Hey, have you just left school? Are you the new boy?"

I hated that, and I also hated the spots that were climbing over my face at the time! Being 16, you don't know whether to think of yourself as a man or a boy. You also don't know if your patter is any good. But that's the thing about living in Glasgow. Others will soon let you know if your patter's crap! Glasgow people can be very funny but they can also cut you to ribbons as quick as they can make you laugh.

There was good and bad points about working in Muirheads. The good were the girls, and there were loads of them working there. The bad was that I only got one Saturday off in four. So what about the Celtic? Exactly. I was going to miss loads of games, and my boss was a Rangers fan! But back to the girls. I had a strong fancy for a girl called Margaret Deeprose. Yes, quite a name!

Margaret came from Easterhouse, and she was a couple of years older than me. Now a girl at 18 is light years ahead of a boy of 16. And didn't she let me know that!

Do you remember that song by Sandie Shaw, called 'Puppet on a String'? That was me, I was the one on the string. Just when I thought I was making an impression on her, she would let me know that she was just kidding me on. But there were others and I soon got my own back on her. You know, walking by unexpectedly with someone else on your arm!

One of my first duties was to empty the Lingerie window of woman's corsets and bras and what not. My understanding of my instructions was that I was to empty the window and bring the lingerie upstairs to the Display department, leaving the naked dummies in the window. What I didn't know was that there was a special method of getting a corset off a dummy, and that you didn't do it in the window in full glare of the street. So imagine the scene. You have this dummy and you have to strip it of it's underwear, and I'm attempting this with people standing outside the window waiting for a bus!

I had the dummy standing on it's head, with me pulling from underneath, with my foot wedged in a delicate part of the dummy's anatomy! I had the dummy on the floor with me pulling from the side, and it wedged against the wall. This was a private battle, and I had to win it, especially with passers-by urging me on from outside the window.

After half an hour and the window strewn with female dummies lying all over the place like dead bodies, I was eventually rescued by one of the senior girls, who had been sent down from the Display department to find out what had happened to me. She tried her best not to laugh, as I explained I just couldn't get the corsets off. The bras were no problem for some reason, but the corsets were doing my head in!

When we worked late and the store was in 80% darkness, they used to say that there was a ghost on the second floor. Just another wee wind-up for the new starts. Can you imagine walking through a huge store with five floors and it's dark? It can be a little bit spooky, even without letting your imagination run away.

After months of this wind-up, I was working late one night, with one other person. I was down on the ground floor carrying dummies up to the fifth. Now, to operate the moving stairs at night you pressed a special button, and turned it off when you got to the top. The girl I'm working with is now down in the window and I'm on my way up the stairs with a couple of stiffs!

I'm on the third floor and on the way up. It's dark and deadly still, at about 9.30 at night. Halfway up and the moving stairs stops. I look up and swear I saw a figure move away. At this point I'm rigid. I mean if I didn't see a figure move away, how come the lift stopped? I decided I wasn't going any further, and I start heading back down the stairs when I hear some movement behind me.

At this point these dummies I was carrying are about to get ditched. I sort of turned around and about 10 feet away from me stood a man wearing a white shirt. The dummies came in quite handy as I was needing them for a bit of comfort.

"What is it?" I ventured.

"Excuse me, do you work here?"

"Aye," I replied.

"I'm looking for the gents department."

"The shop's shut, it closed at 5.30."

"I'm only looking for a gent's coat."

"Right, just wait there, I'll see if I can get someone to help you." I just bolted downstairs, phoned 999 and both me and Maureen locked ourselves in the window until the police came. That was the last time I worked late!

That summer, Celtic reached the Scottish Cup Final against Aberdeen. The Final was to be played on April 11th. It wasn't my turn for a Saturday off, so I asked the boss, Peter Shields, if I could get it off because of the Cup Final. "Afraid not, one of the girls is going to a wedding."

I remember walking through Central Station and having to ask somebody the score. "Three-one to Aberdeen."

A grim score line. I remember wondering what TV channel I'd have to avoid that night!

After about six months I reckoned I wasn't cut out for dressing windows, and my mother came to the rescue.

I was pretty lucky and landed an apprenticeship in silk screen printing. The only reason I got the job in printing was because of my mother. She worked for the SSEB, otherwise known these days as Scottish Power. The company who did the printing for them was called James Best Graphics.

My mother pestered Jim Best, who eventually gave me a start. Jim was a Catholic and a Celtic fan, otherwise I would have had no chance getting into printing, as it is heavy on the Masonic side. I am grateful to both. You know what they say, and it's so true. Get a good start and the rest is up to you.

The great divide was pretty evident, and I make no apologies in mentioning this. Because when I attended day-release that year, at the College of Building and Printing just opposite George Square, there were around 16 first-year apprentices and only two were Catholics, including me. Sectarianism at work was alive and kicking in Glasgow 1970s style.

It would be easy to ignore this now that I'm older, but why should I. This was, and is, important. Young men, clearly because of their creed, were not being given the opportunity to get a start in life, and were being discriminated against. Apartheid is bad enough, but this was happening right on our doorstep.

One of the boys who attended the college with me, and who supported Rangers (one of the 14) is now a manager in one of Glasgow's biggest Screen Printers. I spoke to him recently and jokingly asked him how many Catholics he had on the staff. I was expecting him to say 60/40 in favour of non-Catholics. Firstly he pointed out that his company had 28 workers. He then gave me his answer, and he wasn't joking. "See those two guys up at the back of the factory, holding the brushes, they're a couple of Tims. I told you we employed Catholics." After hearing that I have no reason to believe that 23 years later things have changed any.

I remember standing on the platform at all of the 'Celts For Change' rallies, and always ending the evening with this little saying, "We can be proud of ourselves, and what we have achieved in life, because what we have achieved has been achieved on our own merits. We haven't had to join any secret organisation in life to get where we are today, and that's important to you."

That's your identity, and carry it with you all your life, and you will never go wrong. I think there is a weakness in you if you have to depend on that type of organisation to get on. This is something I will preach to my children, because it matters.

I know a great deal of people, who think this way and they are my type of people. People you can trust, people you can depend upon, people who won't bend to temptation.

Craigie Street Blues

April 12th 1972. Celtic are playing Kilmarnock in the semifinal of the Scottish Cup. I travelled to the match on the supporters bus from Govan Road, which I was beginning to do regularly. At this stage my dad was also starting to go back to games, but usually only to home matches. Thankfully he didn't go to this one I am about to mention. I'm 18 and beginning to act like an 18 year old!

Celtic won 3-1 and Ally Hunter played in goal for Kilmarnock at the time, prior to becoming a Celtic player the following season. Dixie Deans scored two and Lou Macari the other. There were a lot of skinheads around at the time, and Kilmarnock had their fair share of them.

We made our way back to where the buses were parked in Myrtle Park just next to Cathkin Park. We were sitting on the bus waiting for it to fill up and the next thing a bottle smacks off the window just next to where I was seated. A bunch of skinheads were running off and myself and plenty of others on the bus were yelling back at them. An obvious reaction from an 18 year old who has just had a bottle thrown at him. In fact I would say it was a mild reaction.

Seconds later the police arrived and yours truly, along with another guy seated behind me, got arrested.

All the police could see as they arrived was the top of the bus in a commotion. They had apparently been following the skinheads, and, as usual with the cops, "too late" was the cry. No matter how much we protested our innocence, we were still lifted. We were taken down to Craigie Street Police Station in Govanhill and formally charged.

That evening I had an arrangement with a lady a year or two older than myself who lived in Govan and who shall remain nameless. In my pocket was a "packet of three." As I stood watching a line of people being charged I noticed that they had to empty their pockets on the desk as they gave their particulars. At this point I'm about sixth in line, and leaning against a radiator. There was no way I was about to produce a packet of "you know whats" in front of everyone, so down they went behind the radiator.

My parents were informed of my arrest and I was put into a cell with another guy. We introduced ourselves, and professed our innocence to each other. After about 30 minutes another four guys arrived, and about an hour later I was about to suffer a major embarrassment. The policeman on the other side of the door (whom I now know as the turnkey) opened the wee eye slot on the door and shouted, "McGlone. Come over here, I've got a note from yer Mammy."

The entire cell burst out laughing, as I shuffled into the corner to read my mammy's note. This is the last thing I needed, considering the company I was keeping.

It read "Don't worry son, we heard all about it, we spoke to a man on the bus."

Five pairs of eyes were staring at me, and one guy shouted: "Well, what does yer Mammy's note say?"

"Shut it," was my considered, if unwise, response.

And then it was two rounds of "Who are you telling to shut it?" Fortunately the potential aggro soon evaporated.

At about six in the morning we were all taken to the Central Police Station in the Saltmarket. We were put in a huge cell which held about 100 people. Everyone who had been arrested in Glasgow that night was brought here. This was a holding cell before people were sent up to the court for a hearing. No matter what you had been arrested for everyone was brought to this giant cell and held until they were called up for fingerprinting. Therefore you can imagine I was keeping some choice company: rapists, robbers, junkies, men of violence and men of innocence, like myself.

In the corner of this 'hotel room' was a toilet seat. Now just imagine you are in desperate need to sit down on it. Would you, in front of over 80 people? Funny thing, but nobody did for the three hours we were there!

There were all sorts of people arriving in this big cell. Men in business suits, in uniforms, in painters overalls, and no kidding, one guy with a 'Milanda' delivery coat on. One person asked him what he had done, and he replied, "I got caught nicking lead from a roof while I was delivering the bread." Priceless! Around 10.00am we were both called and we pleaded: "Not guilty." We were ordered to appear for trial some months later, having been charged with breach of the peace. I left the Court by the nearest door available, and was delighted just to get out of their clutches. Being ordered around like a criminal all night was no fun.

My mother was waiting at another door, expecting to take me for something to eat. I only found this out as I arrived home to find no one around, and she arrived an hour later. I had at this point still to face my father. When the trial came up it turned into a bit of a pantomime. The Court procedure was such that you sat and watched all the trials, prior to yours being called.

The trial before mine was of a young guy who was brought into Court handcuffed to two policemen. He was charged with breaking into Shawfield Stadium, a dog track and home of Clyde FC. It went along the lines of the accused attempting to break into a watchman's hut inside the stadium, in the middle of the night. Inside the hut were two terrified old men, both in Court, and still looking terrified.

The first old man up gave evidence and identified the accused sitting in the dock. As he gave his evidence he described the accused as looking like a 'wild animal'. The second old man was shaking like a leaf and said much the same, except when it came to identifying the accused. The old man was asked if he saw him in court. He looked around, hesitated, looked around again, and pointed straight at me!

I blurted out in astonishment, and proclaimed my innocence. The Judge told me to stand up and give my name. And then told me to sit down again. Because the old man couldn't or wouldn't identify our alleged hut-breaker, he walked free. Meanwhile, I was found guilty after the Judge believed the statements of the three policemen and I was fined £25. My father was none too happy!

Now from when I delivered newspapers, from the age of 14, the love of my life was a girl who lived down the road from me. Her name was Jackie. Now as they say in the trade "Did you get off with her?" meaning are you going out with her? Well no I wasn't, at that time, but I was, on and off, from around 17. This was a big-time love affair and I could safely say she was my first love.

Jackie was the girl everyone fancied. She was great looking, had great legs. She was also the first class act in the street who cut about in hot pants! Personality? Well if she hadn't been all too aware that she had all of these attributes then perhaps we might well have been together today. But we are not, so I can tell you the story.

We went to chapel together, we sneaked into pubs together, and we got caught in the act together. My mother and her mother were very Catholic, and in my mother's eyes Jackie's lights were very bright. In Jackie's mother's eyes young Matthew here may as well have been a saint. Yes he was that pure! Until that fateful Friday night.

As usual a Friday would consist of meeting up and then going back to her house to play a few records. David Bowie, Alice Cooper, James Taylor. Jackie's mum and dad would be off to bed early and we would fool around and all that entailed.

But that night as we got down to some serious 'winchin', Jackie's mother all of a sudden opened the bedroom door, and I'll never forget those next two minutes.

"Jackie, I don't like you and Matt in the room at this time of night with the light off. Come into the living-room now." The room is still in complete darkness at this point and Jackie to her eternal credit remained very cool. Me, well I didn't move in case her mother picked up any giveaway sounds!

"Okay Mum, we'll be through in a minute."

"No, I said now" and then the light went on. You would have been as well throwing a hand grenade into the room! Her Mother flew in, intent on removing Jackie's long hair from her scalp. I meantime was attempting to make myself presentable to the world, as my heart did a three-minute mile!

Much yelling was thrown in my direction from her mother, and much screaming came from Jackie's direction as her Mum took on a very physical role. Seconds later her dad arrived on the scene. He and I had a great relationship up until this point, and the surprising thing was nothing much changed after this incident.

Her mother shouted out words which explained that we had been in a rather compromising state of affairs when she switched the light on. He in turn walked in my direction and said some comforting words which wouldn't be fair to repeat, and then put his arms around me. The mother came hurtling in our direction, so I swiftly ducked in time but I'm afraid her dad wasn't so lucky!

As she screamed "You, get out, get out!" I promptly removed myself to the living-room quarters, in hindsight, not exactly a good idea. Perhaps a minute later her Mum entered the living-room accompanied by screaming daughter. I'm sitting on the couch trying to look saintly, and I was met with "Aarghh, are you still here, get out!" Or words to that effect. "I thought you meant get out of the room" I replied. What she said next was utterly unrepeatable!

I was extremely concerned that Mrs Mac was going to march up to my mum's house and inform Mary Theresa of the evening's nocturnal happenings. But thankfully she didn't. There were repercussions though. Jackie's mum went to live with one of her daughter's for a fortnight, and Jackie didn't get the music centre she was expecting for her birthday.

From then on in we had secret rendezvous, meeting all over the place in the drizzle and the fog and never anywhere comfortable. Any time I saw her mother approaching I quickly looked out my passport!

About six months later on Christmas Day, Jackie and I were walking down Beltrees Road coming back from 12 o'clock Mass in St James's. Jackie said: "I was speaking to my mum this morning and she said it would be okay if you came up to the house this afternoon, if you want."

I nipped up to my house and unwrapped a present I had for someone else, re-wrapped it and put a tag on it with her mother's name on it. I boldly marched down the road to her house which was about 11 houses away. By the time I climbed the stairs to her living-room I was wishing I was somewhere else.

I entered the room feeling about as welcome as a teetotaller on a stag night! All of her family were present and I could feel all the eyes burning right through me. "Merry Christmas everyone" I said, as I stood there with someone else's Christmas present. I walked over and handed it to her mother and planted a cheeky wee kiss right on her cheek!

I had entered the lion's den and had come out unscathed. Character-building Matthew, character-building.

Saturday May 5th, 1973, and we are playing Rangers in the Scottish Cup Final. Now I don't know about you but I have always felt a bit odd taking a woman to a football match. At the same time there is something I like about it as well. Perhaps it's the identity thing, and you feel the person closest to you should enjoy it the way that you do. That they should experience the same feeling. You know, let's enjoy beating them together, or consoling each other.

Therefore, if you troop out of the ground on a high then she will be on the same high level as you. And if you lose, then you won't get frustrated at her when you arrive home and she doesn't understand why you are so down.

Anyway, on this particular day Jackie was with me and we were going to the game together, therefore no misunderstandings later on. It was one of those drizzly, but mild days and I decided to put on my long leather coat (made to measure of course!) from Skint in Union Street. The trend in Glasgow at that particular time was to wear platform shoes and wear long coats. Skint specialised in long, made-to-measure jobs. Girls wore big leather boots with equally giant heels, and long woollen coats with huge lapels. Belts were in as well, and just to complete the trend, my carefully cultivated side-burns were coming along nicely.

Over 122,000 turned up along with Princess Alexandra. The referee was someone we all recognised as being a 'Mason in the Black' J.R.P. Gordon (Newport on Tay). I for some reason always new where the referee came from when I heard his name. That's why I just mentioned it!

There we were standing on the black ash terracing, on the left hand side of the Celtic end, getting well squashed and soaked at the same time. If there was a cover to be built at Hampden then you could be guaranteed it would be built at the Rangers end first. If they were to spend more money on Hampden then instead of putting up a cover at the Celtic end, they would put concrete on the Rangers end terracing, whilst we stood on a mucky uncovered terracing, totally exposed to the elements.

Celtic were favourites and were going for a seventh title in a row. As Kenny Dalglish said after the game: "We always beat Rangers for pace up front and so we liked to draw them up field a bit, then hit them with quick balls." And that's exactly what Celtic did in the 25th minute.

Dixie Deans twisted past two players and released the ball to Kenny, who was off like a whippet before slipping the ball past Peter McCloy who had left his goal line. This happened at the Celtic end and Kenny raced away in the opposite direction from where we were standing, and over to the Celtic fans on his left. Who cared? That special feeling you get running through your body when Celtic bulge the Rangers net engulfed us all. Jackie meanwhile was getting hugged by more males than she ever knew!

One of the best memories I have of Dalglish was his infectious smile when he scored. He always looked as if he'd just won the pools. The opposition equalised 10 minutes before half-time and it was time to instruct Jackie as to where the pie stand was situated!

At the end of the day we lost this game 3-2 due to the worst goal you will ever see in a Cup Final, scored by Tom Forsyth, who wasn't exactly noted for his skill, and who was aptly named by Tommy Docherty as being better suited to wearing a 'butchers apron' . The game was tied at 2-2 and the ball had just hit the post and was rolling along, rather than over, the line. Forsyth scored with his studs!

That guy had one ugly face as he ran away like a demented stallion! It was time for Jackie to encounter one of my blacker moods. This was a spoiled evening. That's what Celtic have the ability to do to you. And Jackie? Well she had just witnessed her last Celtic game in my company.

Celts are a Riot!

At 18 years of age, I reckon I could safely say I had grown up a young Celt.

So how do we sum up those first formative years as a Celtic supporter, those critically important years when the dye is cast?

Did that brick which almost hit me on my first day at school change my attitude in life, and did it make me bitter in any way towards people who supported that blue jersey, or towards my pals who went to that other school? Without sounding saintly, it did not, and I'm glad it didn't. You can always fervently support your team and hold your important principles without being bitter and twisted.

The inability to do this can turn you into a bigot, and all that does is close your mind to other ways of understanding situations. The Scottish Cup Final of 1980 at Hampden Park displayed Glasgow's simmering sectarianism, through no fault of the Celtic support, who were forced to defend themselves after Celtic had won the game 1-0 in extra time through a George McCluskey strike via a Danny McGrain shot.

As soon as the whistle went the Celtic players headed towards their own crowd as winners normally do. The police presence apparently was down on numbers, as most had gone outside the stadium to control the crowd leaving the game. The Celtic players were over at the East terracing as the fans partied there. In their moment of jubilation a small number of them spilled onto the track, not intent on causing trouble, but only on celebrating with the joyous players.

The Rangers support were sick and couldn't handle us celebrating and that is the only reason this riot started. The authorities can make all the excuses they want, but that's what happened.

The police were unable to control them as they charged across the park. The team meanwhile headed off in the direction of the dressing-room as more Celtic fans piled on to the pitch to support the small amount who had initially spilled on to celebrate the victory.

What took place next was a product of what has always simmered between both sets of supporters. The division was there and it only needed an excuse.

Many supporters who are friends, but support different teams, rarely meet up socially on 'Old Firm' days as the tensions surrounding this fixture are much too intense.

Yet these friends who had no intention of fighting each other that day could quite easily have met on that Hampden turf and got ladled into each other. In any situation in life the last thing you think of when you are deliriously happy and celebrating is having a 'square-go' with somebody. The Celtic support basically got involved in the hands on fighting because they were attacked. We didn't run up to the Rangers fans. They ran towards us as we celebrated.

The SFA in their wisdom took the easy way out and fined both teams £20,000. The lesson here seemed to be: "Don't celebrate as you might upset the opposition." Celtic blamed the lack of police. The police in turn blamed the Celtic players for rushing to the Celtic support in triumph at the end of the game. I don't think I have heard so many cop-outs in my life! Everybody blamed drink, but the Secretary of State for

Scotland, George Younger, preferred to use the police statement to blame the Celtic players (as did Rangers).

In their executive committee report the SFA admitted that the Celtic fans: '…had invaded the track and goal area for the purpose of cavorting around and generally celebrating with the Celtic players who had chosen to run to that end of the stadium, on the final whistle, to demonstrate to their supporters their exuberance of victory. At that stage of events there was nothing violent in the exchanges between players and fans. Rather it was a spontaneous, if misguided, expression of joy."

Of the Rangers support the SFA said: "There was no question of celebration in the minds of the fans who invaded from the West end of the ground. They had violence in mind and no sooner was it offered than it was returned with enthusiasm. The brutal and disgusting scenes which followed, as bottles flew and drunken supporters charged and counter-charged from one end of the field to the other, brought disgrace upon the two clubs concerned, upon Scottish football generally, and were an affront to Scotland as a nation."

The Rangers chairman Rae Simpson claimed, at the time, that a number (unknown) of Catholics (unnamed) were employed by Rangers in "responsible" positions (unspecified), that Glasgow was polarised and this was not Rangers fault.

Desmond White was "appalled" that his Club should continue to be accused of sectarianism, and listed various captains and managers who were non-Catholic. Now I don't think that we had to get drawn into that type of argument. Celtic have always played non-Catholics and why not? We may have been founded to help the Irish Catholics in Glasgow, but that does not mean to say we only employ Catholics. It was approaching the 1990s not the 1690s!

In fact on the day of this riot Celtic had more Protestants in their cup-winning team than they had Catholics. The entire point of the matter is a lot more simple. The reason all the authorities were going around in circles was because they were simply looking for excuses.

Keeping things in perspective, and realising why it happened is not too complicated at all. The bitter rivalry between both factions has been ongoing for longer than we care to remember. The division between both groups has been going on even before that first day at school.

This is Glasgow, the West of Scotland, Celtic and Rangers supporters. With that concoction, did the authorities expect anything less than what happened?

It is very easy in this environment to pull the trigger and let loose the sectarian bile, and that is exactly what happened later that year in November. The World Lightweight title fight was to take place at the Kelvin Hall in Glasgow, between the reigning champion Jim Watt and an American called Sean O'Grady.

The known sympathies of some of Watt's supporters, and the suspicious-sounding name of the challenger gave this fight a sectarian edge. However, the way I see it is that if this fight had taken place anywhere apart from Glasgow and certain parts of Ireland, then the sectarian issue would never have been brought to the fore.

'The Celtic View' editor at the time approached the promoter Mickey Duff concerning a promotional visit to Celtic Park. In the event, Watt couldn't make it because he was training in London at the time. Therefore it was left to O'Grady to attend the Celtic/Kilmarnock match himself.

As is normal with most celebrities, O'Grady was presented with a Celtic jersey as a souvenir of his visit and he put it on. Some say he was misguided, I reckon it was displayed in an innocent fashion. What is the problem in wearing it in front of the Celtic crowd? But the sight of a Celtic jersey on O'Grady was perceived as flaunting the Club's colours. The final irony for all of the bigots who attempted to give Celtic a hard time over this was that O'Grady, despite his name, was not a Catholic, and was, in fact, a member of the Millwood Baptist Church in Oklahoma City, USA. Talk about jumping the gun. It was further evidence that in this part of the world, even a name can stir up the pot of simmering sectarianism that we all experience in our daily life.

As we move on in life our passion for our Club won't leave many of us. And although we may live in other parts of the world to enable us to earn a living, we are only separated by miles, land and oceans, but never in spirit.

You may change as a person as the years wear on, but whether you live in Toronto or Tahiti, barely a day will go by when you won't have a wee Celtic recall in your mind. A flash from the past. And for those few moments you will drift away in your own personal dream. Now surely that proves our love is far more than just a football team. They are you and you are them.

Was it our parents that made us this way or was it the streets we grew up on? Do you remember all of the things you were never taught in the house, but which you learned outside as you roamed around like a street urchin. Often you discovered things that were unspoken about indoors, but you were expected to learn about outdoors. Did your parents ever tell you anything about the facts of life? Mine never did. I think we could safely say that by far and large the majority of us were left to find out by our own devices. It was far too embarrassing for them, and ultimately too cringing for us! You would have made more facial movements in the other direction in those sweaty moments, than you would ever have done previously if you were told to sit down and listen to your dad. Well I assume it would be your dad! So was it your parents or the streets who made you addicted to the Celts? Let me offer you a few scenarios. If you were born in Glasgow then I reckon it was a combination. Firstly, your choice of school had a major bearing. I will run examples side by side which may offer a guideline.

I will compare Glasgow to Toronto. Two brothers are brought up in Glasgow and one has emigrated around the mid-sixties. Both are steeped in the Celtic tradition. Both have children. The Glasgow child kicks a ball around and reads and hears Celtic through the newspapers and television, and plays out his fantasies on those important streets of life.

The Toronto child looks at the Celtic photos on the wall that have been put there by his father. The child listens to music that is of an Irish/Scots tradition, and listens to the father speak in a tongue that is Gaelic and not what he hears out on Sun Valley Avenue.

The ball on the Avenue is mostly thrown rather than kicked, and is also a different shape. The child walks through the mosquito trap door and eventually out the main door to witness his father with his head on the kitchen table, banging his fist, his face contorted as he listens to the World Service radio giving a commentary on the game from Glasgow.

He is hitting highs and lows by the minute, and he is an emotional mess 3,000 miles away from where the game is being played. The child walks back out into the yard and wonders what is wrong with his father as he glances across to his friend, Brad, who is playing happily with Mom and Dad as they relax, enjoying the barbecue.

"Why can't my Dad be like Brad's and have a barbecue on a Saturday? Why has he got to be so unapproachable, with the radio strapped to his ear? Why can't he be like other Dads and do their type of things? Why does he all of a sudden jump about all over the kitchen or shout names at the radio, or tell my Mom to be quiet? He grabbed me last week and shouted: 'Yes Patrick wee man! We done it, that's us three points ahead of the Huns.' I'm still trying to work it all out, and he still won't take me to see the Toronto Blue Jays in the Sky Dome."

This won't happen in all cases but it does prove that because it is not evident on the street and it's not in the papers or on the telly, those formative years in a different environment can have a telling effect on those Celtic emotions.

There are opposites to the above though, and an example of this is a young Canadian girl born to Scottish parents who emigrated from Glasgow to Canada in the mid-sixties. She like her father is steeped in Celtic and their traditions. Her brother though, has no interest.

Stephanie Langan and her father Jim attend the Bramalea CSC in Toronto, Canada. This club is fully-equipped to beam in games from Celtic Park and this they do on a regular basis. They are not short on commitment either. The club has bought season tickets in the investor section at Celtic Park and has invested heavily in shares.

Stephanie and her dad are shareholders and Jim's passion has obviously rubbed off on his daughter. Stephanie crossed the Atlantic (not for the first time) in September 1995 to attend the Cup Winners Cup tie against Dinamo Batumi, and the game against Rangers a few days later.

I took her down to the Celtic shrine in Glasgow's Calton District, Bairds Bar. Now if you have never been in this pub you have missed out on a bastion of Celticness!

As she scanned around the walls and ceiling which are totally covered in Celtic photos and memorabilia, I had to ask her why she felt so strongly about the Club and its traditions. It does seem a bit unusual, a girl from Canada and an accountant by day being so interested in what we cherish so dearly.

She said it was her father's teachings, the traditional music that was played at home, and everything about Irish history that held her interest, and all of this combined with what Celtic are all about and what makes a Celtic follower. This attracted her from 3,000 miles away.

When choosing a husband she would prefer him not to be Canadian. "Somebody from Ireland or Scotland, somebody who understands what I'm interested in. I used to go out with a Korean/Canadian but I would prefer somebody from my own culture."

That kind of commitment is commendable, and is the kind of thing which ensures our culture flourishes even further across the seas. No matter where we are in the world the Celtic beat ticks and us with it.

Jock Stein the Immortal Father

When the news announcer said "Jock Stein is dead" I really didn't need him to tell me that. I knew Jock was dead, and I don't mean that in any flippant manner. It's just that when you think you know someone that well (but I didn't know him personally at all) you seem to have this sixth sense and your instinct takes over and that feeling becomes reality.

Jock was a very powerful man, physically and mentally, and even the smallest of glimpses on TV when he had fallen at the mouth of the tunnel at Ninian Park, Cardiff, told me the worst. Men like Jock wouldn't fall over unless there was a serious problem. If I take myself back to the evening of 10 September 1985 I can remember the events as though they happened yesterday.

On the pitch Scotland needed a point to go into a two-match play-off against the winners of the Australasian section and then qualify for the World Cup Finals in Mexico the following year.

I will be honest with you. Scotland as a football team really don't do very much for me. I reckon it goes back to the 1960s and 70s when Celtic players were booed by fans who were there to support Scotland but couldn't stomach the sight of a Celtic man in the dark blue. That sickened me.

If Jimmy Johnstone was playing then they chanted for Willie Henderson; if Davie Hay was playing they chanted for Sandy Jardine who would be sitting on the bench. I recall one game when the Rangers end started their incessant chanting for Jardine, and Bobby Brown, the Scotland manager at the time, cravenly bowed to their prejudices and brought off Davie Hay much to the delight of the majority of the Scotland crowd. That was the last straw for me as a Scotland fan.

In Cardiff that evening in 1985 Jock seemed to be in a very relaxed mood as he walked over the pitch prior to kickoff. During shoot-in practice the Scottish crowd refused to return the balls to the Welsh keeper, Neville Southall. He in turn enlisted the aid of Stein who motioned to the crowd to return the balls. One came flying out and then another. Southall suggested there was a third, but Stein appeared to make it clear that two out of three from the Scottish crowd was not bad going! Jock ended up with his arms around the Welsh keeper's shoulders having a friendly chat as they left the field.

When Davie Cooper scored for Scotland with nine minutes left the entire visitors' bench leapt into the air, but Jock sat motionless - the first sign that perhaps all was far from well. As the minutes ticked away a photographer encroached nearer the bench with his obtrusive lens. Jock became agitated by this and jumped from the bench to physically move him.

As I sat at home watching the game the cameras all of a sudden swung over to the touchline and Stein was being carried up the tunnel by a policeman. It was hard to comprehend at the time what was actually happening.

My knowledge of what happened in the next half has obviously been borne to me sometime after the event. Apparently for those 30 minutes the medical team worked frantically to try to revive the Big Man's heart. When no response was forthcoming the procedure was terminated.

During that time which seemed a lot longer than just 30 minutes I paced around the house with the TV and radio on, wondering what was happening and when we would hear something definite. Soon after came the announcement that Jock had died. For the first minute or so I showed no emotion. I just sat glued to the screen perhaps hoping for them to say it was a mistake.

I am not very good at displaying emotions, but on this occasion I just broke down, just as I did when my Mum told me over the phone that my Dad had died. There were two older men in my life whom I had the utmost respect for: Jock and my Dad, although my Father, probably like many others in the West of Scotland, probably died without knowing about that love from his son. Now the two men who meant the most to me in my life were gone.

I have often asked myself why this event elicited such an emotional response from me. And it's really quite easy. The source of all my happiest childhood memories was Celtic FC and the fantastic achievements they had with Jock Stein at the helm. He was the catalyst for these events, the happiest days of my life as a Celtic supporter.

It would be difficult to say exactly when he became a presence in my life. As a child of 10 you tend to be more interested in the players than the manager. But at the back of your mind was the awareness that Jock Stein was the boss and was worthy of the utmost respect.

Stein was one of those people who learnt the hard way. His formative years were spent in a tough environment. One where if you had the mere basics of life you respected them as they probably represented everything you had. Respect was a big feature in the 1920s and 30s, when Stein would be running around the streets of Burnbank, Hamilton, in Lanarkshire. Kids today would shudder at the thought of having to live in those times. No cinemas, no replica football tops, no trendy trainers with air bubbles fitted into the soles of their shoes, no computer games.

Stein arrived as manager at Celtic Park on March 10, 1965 and his last duty as manager of Hibernian was to remove Rangers from the Scottish Cup and save Celtic the trouble of doing it later. At that time Celtic's record since the end of WW2 was pretty grim. The 20 years since 1945 had produced the miserable total of one League Championship, two Scottish Cups and two League Cups and that was from 60 competition entries.

When Jock returned to Celtic as manager he said "If I can achieve for Celtic what I achieved for Hibs, then I feel I will have done well for them." The term understatement was invented for such an utterance! A firm belief instilled in him from his days in the Lanarkshire pits and a straightforward way of applying it would bring this man success we could never have dreamed of.

Within six weeks of his arrival Jock delivered the Scottish Cup, which forms one of my earliest Celtic memories. You could send 2/6d into the Evening Citizen and in return you would receive a black and white photo with the team in all their glory holding Billy McNeill aloft with the cup. That picture was up on my wall for years, and I think it was then that I realised we were a bloody good team and that this man Stein was a bit of a dude!

In the very same year 'The Celtic View' was introduced for the first time and Stein said: "Have the first issue ready for the week after the Cup Final and leave a blank space on page one for a picture of the boys with the Cup."

Stein was not a boaster, but maybe this was an early show of the man's confidence.

He was never one to mess about, and in his first year in charge he freed no fewer than 20 players. I spoke to Lisbon Lion Jim Craig who told me that his father ran out to the shops on a Sunday for a newspaper to see if his son was one of the list of frees.

Such a radical approach was characteristic of Stein's whole ethos. In the summer of 1965 Stein was asked to look after the Scotland squad on a temporary basis following Ian McColl's departure, an arrangement that Celtic were remarkably acquiescent about. There were a few provisos though, as Celtic sought to protect their investment.

(a) Wherever a conflict of interest arose, Celtic must come first.
(b) There would be no scouting. (This also recognised the continuing function of the selection committee).

(c) There would be no further approach from the SFA for his services in a similar capacity.

In my opinion Celtic were being very hospitable towards the SFA when they didn't have to be, but at the same time making it quite clear Stein was remaining at Celtic Park, long term.

As Stein pointed half his body in the direction of Scotland's international team, his better half, was engaged in putting Rangers out of the League Cup 2-1. And low and behold we also managed to get two penalties which, although rare today, was even more of a rarity then!

Stein would say "I think it's important to win a match, but I think what is even more important is the manner in which you win." How many managers today could honestly say the same? In 1966 Celtic won the league for the first time since 1954, the year I was born. So there I was, 11 and a wee half, and my team were league champions. You'd better believe I was doing some gloating! If I could transport my feeling then to today, for my twin sons and daughter (aged 14 and 16) to experience I would gladly do so but that is out of my power. That responsibility is in the hands of Tommy Burns and if he delivers the League Championship in '96 or '97 then he had better watch out because I am going to plant a kiss right on his cheek! The nine must be protected. It is unthinkable that Rangers equal or, God forbid, surpass that achievement.

How do you describe a man like Stein in comparison to what others are achieving today? Jock didn't attempt to buy the European Cup. He won it with guile, craft, awareness, ability, expertise, knowledge, common sense and the confidence to preach that you are good enough to do it. One of the most heartwarming things I ever heard Jock say was "The most pleasure any manager can get is seeing everyday boys joining the Club as youngsters and growing into men and giving themselves a better social standing than they could ever have dreamed of previously."

That kind of comment comes from someone who nurtures a natural concern for other people's welfare. The sort of thing your father would perhaps say, or think. I think open emotion in statements like that are very much part of the reason Stein was so successful as a manager. I mean, if I was a boy at Celtic trying to mature into a senior professional and I heard that, I would burst a gut in every way possible to repay that sort of care and concern. He was much more than a football manager, he was a psychologist as well.

Nevertheless, despite all of this the conclusion is inescapable that he was treated in a pretty tawdry manner at the end of his reign at Celtic Park.

As I mentioned earlier, when I was about 14 years of age I was lucky enough to get a trial for Celtic Boys Club. As I pointed out, before you even got a trial with the Boys Club you had to train for about a month just to get fit. The way I looked at it was: you were there for a month, so whether you were duff or not at least you had been there. You had experienced that wee bit of Celticness. I think some fans will know just what I'm talking about. It might sound a wee bit daft, but it matters.

So there we were, running around the Parkhead car park under the guidance of Jim Torbett and who appeared but Mr Stein himself. Now, if I didn't run into the guy in front of me, then I ran into the guy next to him. At that moment all I could think of was that he might just be looking at ME!

He might just say "Hey son, come over here a wee minute, you look pretty nifty." A friend of mine, and one just as emotionally attached to Celtic as I, Jim Stevenson, told me that when he was a kid kicking the ball against the railings outside his house he always stared up at his nearest neighbour's window and when he saw his neighbour looking out of the window the young Stevenson imagined it was big Jock looking at him. This inspired him to improve his technique and put a wee glow in his heart. I can identify so easily with that as I'm sure many others can. Alas, my dreams in that direction were never to be fulfilled. Even when I thought he was walking over towards me, he was really only walking to his car. Still that's better than nothing, or have I just lost the plot?

Another great man, Bill Shankly, said of Stein "If he has useful players he trains them the right way, and he encourages them to do what they are best at, not to mention the other wee things you need in your game. Jock would then merge all these things together. It's a form of socialism - without the politics of course."

Many of the successful managers today were connected to Jock in some way or another. Alex Ferguson at Manchester United, Kenny Dalglish at Blackburn. Both have won the English Premiership, while Billy McNeill, Davie Hay and Tommy Burns have all won major trophies as managers and all played under Stein when they were wee bhoys. So unless this is some kind of strange coincidence, the magic has indeed rubbed off.

It has been common knowledge for quite a while now that Manchester United tried to poach Stein via Matt Busby. Jock did indeed think about it, though not for long, and stated later: "Yes I have had opportunities to move which would have been better financially for me, but I have ties here. The most important tie for me is, I like being the manager of Celtic. I also like the people who support us. I want them to get a bit of success. "

'A bit of success?' We almost overdosed on it! Life then as a Celtic fan was sheer bliss, and giving Rangers a doing on a regular basis was something money couldn't buy. Times were so good in that period and perhaps human nature made us take those halcyon days for granted. My recurring nightmare is that Rangers do the nine. I have dreamed about it and I wake up totally depressed and in a cold sweat.

I think the reason for this is that you feel it belongs to you. It has become so interwoven within Celtic folklore that the prospect of your greatest rivals coming up the path to take it away from you before laughing at you forever in the process is scary.

I am glad Jock doesn't know what is going on today and that he has been spared the agony of Rangers getting close to his remarkable achievement.

There were many players who didn't make it under Stein, most whom you will never have heard of. But many did do the business for Celtic. Paul Wilson, for example. Most fans under the age of 17 will probably never have heard of him, but he was a big part of Stein's plans in the 1970s. Does anyone know what he is doing today? I certainly don't, and I would love to know what became of him.

I go into Bairds Bar on occasion and I see Bertie Auld, a Lisbon Lion, serving young and old a pint or a half and I don't feel comfortable with that. I don't want Bertie to serve me a pint or a bottle of Bud. I want to see him sitting in a castle in some luxury, with his wife and his children and their children, putting his feet up and wallowing in his achievements.

We are talking about heroes here, not just ordinary people. I'd love to know what went wrong in these cases. Were they underpaid? Were they a bit naive with their money? All I know is that I don't want them fetching me pints. I want to remember them as they are on those posters on my wall.

I recall walking into Heraghtys Bar around 1991 and another Lisbon Lion was sitting propped up on the bar with a big hat and a borrowed coat on, singing his heart out. "For God's sake," I thought, "get him down from there." I'm sorry if you think that these people should not be protected from this type of exposure, but I just happen to believe they are a bit special, and I would prefer them to remain that way.

On Monday May 9th, 1966, two days after clinching Celtic's first League Championship for 12 years, Jock said: "It is up to us, to everyone at Celtic Park now, to build up our own legends. We don't want to live with history, to be compared to legends of the past. We must make new legends and our League Championship win is the first step towards doing that." Stein could never have imagined how prophetic a statement that would turn out to be. It is uncanny how often he made these kind of statements that contained a sort of wisdom that would transcend changing times and circumstances.

In Jock's finest hour, the Lisbon triumph, he suddenly got up off the bench moments before the final whistle and walked away alone. At the start of that magnificent season, before his team had entered any competition, he told his players: "This can be a year that everyone of us can remember, so let's make sure that each player helps each other. Make sure if someone is having a bad game somebody near him helps him out."

Twelve months later he had won the European Cup, Scottish League Championship, Scottish Cup, League Cup and Glasgow Cup. That will never be equalled again.

Jock's final trophy for Celtic was the 1977 Scottish Cup, as Rangers were beaten 1-0 in the final. At the end of the game Stein and Kenny Dalglish ran towards each other, greeting each other with a handshake and a hug. I can still see it today, a wonderful moment for all who were there to savour.

The following year the Celtic versus Liverpool testimonial match was arranged for Jock at Parkhead. When he walked onto the pitch to receive his accolade from the support his 'Lisbon Lions' team were waiting on the centre circle for him, waiting to receive the master, the 'Big Man', the man who made all of them heroes.

I feel Jock was not properly recognised by the Celtic Board at the time of his departure. Considering his achievements he should have been offered a very senior position and never been allowed to leave. He was offered a directorship with responsibilities to "...help develop the commercial side of things at Celtic." But if Stein had taken up this offer it would have been something of a comedown for a man of his stature, abilities and leadership qualities.

You should never have to invent a job for a legend, and I would hate to think that a higher position wasn't offered to him because of his religion. There is a photograph taken in the boardroom when Billy McNeill became manager in succession to Jock. It shows Desmond White's outstretched hand clasping that of Billy McNeill, with Jock relegated to the background, looking, and no doubt already feeling, like an outcast. As I became older I realised the significance of his expression. Now I cannot even bare to look at it. That picture is living testimony to the shame of everyone connected with the shoddy way in which Jock was treated.

Over the years I have become more informed regarding the circumstances regarding Jock's departure from Celtic Park. In many ways it reads like a horror story. According to Jock himself, "there was one member of the Board who said it would be, 'over his dead body' if Jock Stein was ever to be made a director of the Club."

Jock's wife Jean said: "I was sitting outside in the car with Lady Kelly when John (Jock) was talking to the directors about what was going to happen at Celtic Park. John walked over to the car and said to both of us: 'You'll never guess what they want me to do.' Neither of us had the slightest idea. 'They want me to sell pools tickets.' He then kind of smiled and said that they also wanted him to become a director, that this was a suggestion."

Jean continued: "Lady Kelly, who knows more about Celtic Football Club than almost anyone, told him it would not happen. She just said there and then that John would never get a seat on the Board. She was absolutely right."

Jock's daughter Ray said: "That whole business, the way it was handled, hurt my dad to the bone. To some extent it broke him. It was like someone close to him dying, or even like something dying inside him. Eventually he got over it a bit."

Jock's son George said: "To be offered the Commercial Manager's job was shocking. He looked on that as an insult. The fact that these people offered him something like that showed they didn't know the kind of man they were dealing with. Or, if they did, then they knew this was the way to get rid of him. Quite honestly he just didn't think it worthwhile arguing with the type of people who thought he would make a pools agent, possibly a glorified pools agent. He didn't want to dignify people like that by fighting with them. If Sir Robert Kelly had been alive he would probably have become a director."

Does reading that not make you feel physically sick? Winning 25 major trophies and being treated like a ticket vendor. Words fail me!

Jock's last salary at Celtic Park in 1977 was £12,100. Let me give you an even clearer picture of the type of people we had here. When Jock almost lost his life in a car accident in 1975 he was off work for a year. He won his settlement against the driver of the other car. What did Celtic do? When the settlement was finalised the Club took back the wages they had given him for that year when he was sick.

I know all of this makes very depressing reading, but if you didn't know it before you are aware of it now.

Another of the disgraceful actions of the old Board was in 1989 when they refused to accept a bronze bust of Stein, commissioned and paid for by Celtic supporters. The man behind the pioneering Celtic fanzine 'Not The View', Gerry Dunbar, came up with the idea and the Celtic Board refused to accept it. In effect they were rejecting a gift from Celtic supporters offered in appreciation of Jock Stein's achievements for the Club. Something the Celtic Board were incapable of doing themselves. Through NTV the support had a voice and the Board did not like it.

The people who had subscribed to the fund for the commissioning of this work of art were branded 'malcontents' by the then Chairman Jack McGinn and his self-serving cronies on the Board and the bust eventually found a grateful and appreciative home at the world famous People's Palace in nearby Glasgow Green. Present at the handing-over ceremony were Jock's Daughter Ray and his assistant, Sean Fallon, and a dozen or so fans including yours truly. Happily, under the new Board the bust found it's way to its real home, Celtic Park, six years later in September 1995.

In August, 1995 myself and a friend, Mark Graham, founded the Jock Stein Immortal Celtic Supporters Club. We have closed the membership at 100 members. The Club's motto is: "To support Celtic and have fun." In my own small way it is a personal thanks to a man who gave me fantastic moments as a Celtic fan. Memories I have carried as a child and adult.

Away Days in Europe

Sporting Lisbon 19.10.83

The one thing you are guaranteed when you travel abroad with the Celtic support are characters who have the ability to put you in stitches, and I don't mean the type you get in the casualty unit!

There are certain lads who go through their life with the ability to see a funny side to everything. One of these jesters is fairly well-known to many at Celtic. Step forward the inimitable Charlie Devlin. Now Charlie likes a drink, and that isn't a euphemism for something more serious. But he knew when to stop, especially when he began, gradually of an evening, to adopt a more horizontal than vertical posture, and to display his own peculiar gift of tongues! And on these foreign trips, like many of us, he enjoyed his little libation that wee bit more extravagantly. As soon as I noticed him in the departure lounge at Glasgow Airport en route to Lisbon, I thought of a story which had filtered back to Glasgow from the previous round of this tournament.

Five weeks earlier, Celtic had played away from home in

the first round of the UEFA Cup against the Danish side Aarhus. The setting of the tie in one of the most picturesque parts of Denmark was enough to inspire our Charles to new lyrical heights. After a gruelling bus journey from Glasgow, he duly hit the streets of Aarhus and was seen marching down the main road chanting "Aarhus in the middle of the street, Aarhus in the middle of our street," to the tune of the chart hit by Madness! Charlie, you may have guessed, also made a cameo appearance on our trip to Lisbon.

As away days went the Lisbon jaunt was a considerable one in terms of cost. Leaving Glasgow around 11.00am on the Monday, half of the passengers suddenly became uncharacteristically camera-shy as STV filmed the fans boarding the plane. This, I'm certain, was not unrelated to them having just picked up their fortnightly government pay-cheques courtesy of the DHSS. Not unnaturally they were less than enthusiastic about alerting Her Majesty's welfare agents!

The Hotel Penta in Lisbon was the most impressive I have stayed in on any European trip, but it was distressingly close to one of Portugal's biggest shanty towns. I took a walk over to the camp and I doubt I will ever see such scenes of deprivation and squalor again.

The following day some friends and I visited Lisbon's town centre. The first thing we did was pop into a local barber for a shave. And I can assure you this was one of the few times I will let a punter who resembled a Mexican bandit hold an open razor so near to my throat! Later, as we went in search of a beer, we again witnessed a sight which made me think of what desperate people will do just in order to survive.

As we walked down the street a woman sat begging on the pavement holding a young child who had a hand and a foot missing. I must admit at first I thought of how heartbreaking it must have been for the parents to have a child born in such a tragic state. It was only later, back at the hotel, that the staff informed us that some people in the shanty towns will deliberately mutilate their children and thus raise their sympathy profile in the eyes of strangers.

That evening we went downtown in search of one of

Lisbon's better bars. The one we chose had a dazzling array of pretty girls sitting at the bar. Now I am not trying to make excuses here and pretend that I walk about with blades of grass protruding from my ears, but I had no idea that these delectable young women were having their tea-break from the rigours of their nocturnal trade!

So there I was, Mr Streetwise from Glasgow, and these nubile young girls were asking me where I came from and what I worked at. I genuinely believed they were interested in me as a person and wanted to make conversation. Instead they were only interested in the Escudos in my pocket! Now I will not portray myself as an example of moral rectitude. I'm not, but nor am I in the habit of parting with my pennies for something I have never paid for before. So as I ordered another pot of the local brew I just had to wait for the lads to join me after their five minutes of being transported to the heights of shady passion!

The following day we thought we would try to get ahead of the pack, so four of us ordered a taxi to the Holy of Holies, the Estadio Nacional, where Celtic won the European Cup on May 25, 1967. You know the saying, 'when in Rome, do as the Romans do'? Well as Tims in Lisbon, we had to do what Tims have to do!

Our taxi pulled up outside the stadium which is now used mostly as a municipal sports ground for schoolchildren. Just being able to stand there with the sun behind us, was awe-inspiring; at last looking upon the scene of our greatest achievement.

If you were to ask a Celtic fan why he is so in love with his club, these surroundings would enable him to reach deeply into his soul and produce his most meaningful explanation.

For a supporter who wasn't at the final then this is the best and nearest he will ever get to experiencing that "I was there" feeling. If you ever go to Lisbon get yourself a taxi to this Mecca. It's well worth the time and effort. Stage two for us was to gain access to the pitch but standing in our way was a gardener, complete with pitchfork, labouring amongst the shrubbery.

So with the shrine immediately in front of us our only obstacles were a wee man about 70 years old and a fence you could have easily scaled when you were ten. My instinct told me to approach this in Hercule Poirot mode and to dispense with the Harrison Fords! "Excuse me, we are Celtic supporters from Scotland. We played here many years ago. Can we please come in for two minutes?" Once we were over that fence the two minutes could be expanded into an hour, no danger!

"Ah, Zeltics, I know them, ze are good team, I remember."

I replied, "We would like to come in, can we please?"

"No, no ees not possible."

At this point I was beginning to despair, but at the same time we had to get in. With a pile of Escudo notes emerging from my pocket, our gardener's eyes started to show some signs of life!

After our last pleading gesture our man relented but made it quite clear we were not to stand on his grass. And we didn't, at least not until his back was turned! After about 15 minutes he went for a tea break as we meandered harmlessly behind the goal. But when he disappeared out of sight we had the place all to ourselves so onto the pitch we careered, our bellies bouncing around! And for those moments we were the Lisbon Lions. We crossed balls with pinpoint accuracy and headed powerfully into the goal and we turned to the cheering multitudes. It's only we Celtic fans who can play for Celtic with a beer belly, score a goal without a ball and turn to a crowd who aren't there and then go home experiencing the best buzz ever and still reckon we are normal! It's a disease and we don't want a cure.

The game

One of the strange things about football is that over the years it can throw up so many unexpected scenarios. For example, the Celtic team on the evening of this game had Jim Melrose and Mark Reid playing (where are they now?); Pat Bonner and Paul McStay, who are still playing for Celtic; Tommy Burns, Roy Aitken and Murdo MacLeod who are

Premier Division managers; Willie McStay who is Celtic youth coach and Brian McClair who could be doing a job for us now; Davie Provan, meanwhile, has become a prince of the airwaves.

The game itself was rather grim. Celtic were lucky, I thought, only to lose 2-0. But if we are honest with ourselves, we don't go on these trips primarily to watch the 90 minutes. It's more of an exploration trip with your pals: enjoy the sunshine; make friends with the locals; enjoy the odd shandy and play the part of being an ambassador for your country. A sort of cultural attache, if you like!

The stadium itself was pretty much a concrete bowl with sparse cover in the posher areas. As far as segregation goes, yes, they did have an area for the Celtic fans but in their wisdom they decided to throw in a couple of hundred mental Portuguese fanatics, just for a laugh!

When the local police finally decided to do something about the segregation, our main concern was not really the game. It was more a case of watching that you didn't get belted on the back of the head with a lump of ice the size of a half-brick. The police literally stood and watched the local fans take turns to nip up to the beer bar and help themselves to large lumps of ice which were used to keep the bottled beer cold.

During this period I stood and watched a Celtic fan and a Sporting fan attempting communication through the main segregation meshed fence. The Sporting fan seemed to be gesticulating to our guy that if they both climbed up to the top of the fence then they could enjoy a drink together from the bottle the Celtic fan held, and this they both did.

As I watched with interest, they both reached the top around the same time, with the fence being around 12ft high. At this point the Celtic man handed over the bottle, in a friendly sort of Scottish New Year fashion. As soon as the Portuguese fan finished drinking from the bottle he promptly smashed it over the Celtic man's skull. He in turn slid down the mesh fence in a sort of Tom and Jerry style pose as the Sporting fan headed off into his own crowd. So much for the cultural attache bit!

In certain European countries, in my experience mostly around the Mediterranean areas, the police don't really have much of a clue how to organise and segregate crowds or how to spot potential trouble. Although once it starts they are good at ganging up in groups of four or five and sticking the boot and baton into one individual.

Leaving Sporting's stadium proved this point to me. I witnessed at least two of our fans being struck by Sporting fans. When they complained to the police they were promptly struck again, this time by the cops!

Being outnumbered 15 to 1 by a shower of mad Portuguese while the police stood by was a scary scenario. But come the hour, come the man. Enter stage right the bold Charlie Devlin!

As we made it back on to the bus, we were still being hounded by these brave Sporting savages.

Now Charlie has found himself in some strange circumstances. Once when the Scottish Cup was visiting Heraghtys Bar in the 1980s, Charlie was found with the plinth on his knee and armed with a 10 pence piece attempting to remove any sign of the name 'Rangers' on the Cup. Rangers' name is not actually on the Trophy, the last name inscribed on the Cup being Celtic in 1901.

One of Charlie's other awkward but more serious moments was when he was out and about one Halloween night and left Heraghtys dressed up as a nurse, complete with the obligatory bra and suspenders. As he left the pub slightly inebriated he was hit by a car as he attempted to cross the road. The far from funny side was that he suffered serious leg and pelvic injuries. But there he was, lying on a trolley in the casualty unit at the Victoria Infirmary while a nurse offered him a comforting hand, patting him on the head with the consoling words, "Don't worry hen, you'll be seen to shortly" - only to discover a grizzly moustache as she ran her hand over his face and turned his (her) head around!

But back to Lisbon. As we sat on the coach I must admit to feeling relatively safe after our experience on leaving the ground, but not for long. As the mob outside danced around the coach like Apaches on firewater, suddenly a brick came flying through the window. It was curtains drawn and heads down as low as we could put them, but not for Charlie and his mate Mick Gilligan from Belfast. They had decided enough was enough and they both attempted to jump off the coach and 'get intae' the first available Portuguese aggressor.

Outside the coach it was like a scene from Zulu Dawn as they danced around us. But both Charlie and Mick had absorbed enough provocation and it was only when they were physically pulled back by half a dozen others that the bus finally managed to pull away. But the crazed locals in the stadium apart, the Portuguese were very friendly. And nothing that happened at the game will ever sully the memory of paying homage at the shrine called the Estadio Nacional. Since I was a boy aged 12 this place has held a special place in my heart. When the family were all sitting around the telly, curtains drawn in the back room of our Pollok home, watching Celtic winning the European Champions Cup I vowed I would visit that place one day and stand where Billy McNeill stood to hold the Cup aloft. Sixteen years later I did, and it was magic!

Dinamo Kiev 5.11.86

I always thought there was something strange about having to visit a small office above a chip shop in Glasgow's Bath Street to get to a football match in Russia.

Celtic were about to play the second leg of their European Cup tie against the champions of Russia, Dinamo Kiev. The Club had chartered a plane and to make up the cost they invited supporters to fly with the team. For some reason Celtic Secretary Chris White wanted to know all the names of the fans who were travelling. Perhaps he was worried that just as 'perestroika' was beginning to become established in Russia, some of us may have been of a mind to re-establish the Cold War.

For most of us it was a bit of a thrill to travel abroad with the players, especially to such a mysterious and remote city as Kiev. Russia has always held a mysterious allure for me. Maybe it was something to do with James Bond and Harry

Palmer movies but I found myself looking forward to this trip more than others!

The nuclear accident at Chernobyl had occurred only a few months prior to the scheduled date of the game and the press had a field day as players, management and directors were duly called upon to voice their concerns about safety.

But obscure men in grey suits from even more obscure-sounding government safety departments assured us that all would be fine. All the same, though, Celtic and most of their fans took no chances and decided to take along their own food. For many, myself included, that meant a quick trip to the food hall at Littlewoods to stock up with pre-packed sandwiches, pies, sausage rolls, bridies and crisps; all those foodstuffs that make up the staple diet of your average healthy Timaloy!

But if our fears were allayed somewhat with the nuclear reassurances our consternation increased on first glimpse of the Aeroflot Aircraft that was expected to carry us halfway round the world. It looked as if it would have been rejected at auditions for the Wacky races!

Any hopes we may have entertained about sitting anywhere near the players were quickly dispelled as a curtain, similar to the drapes that hung in your mum's house in the 1960s, separated the stars from the plebs. The curtain could be seen as an apt symbol of the contempt the directors had for the fans in those days.

Let's just say that the flight was best forgotten although I'm sure I was not the only passenger who felt, at certain times, that wee bit closer to God. It's on trips like these that the airline companies should lay on the services of a padre! In Kiev four and a half hours later we encountered customs and passport control officers who made Jim Farry look like a lovable rogue. An optimistic fan in front of me had a cassette of Bruce Springsteen's "Born in the USA" in his hand luggage. If he had been wearing a slogan saying "The Kremlin Politburo are all corrupt, capitalist running-dogs" he would have got a better reception from the officer who simply took the cassette and started to pull the tape out of the reel!

The hotel itself was a bit of a skyscraper and better than what I had expected. Mistake number one: let's change some money! Fairly straightforward you might imagine, but nobody knew how many Russian notes you could get for sterling. As things turned out the guys who were at the back of the queue thought they were the lucky ones. Lurking around the corner were a group of Libyans who were offering you 4 times as many Russian notes as the official desk would hand over.

Lesson number two. For those of us Rockefellers who thought we had just cut a nice wee deal a short sharp pain was to be inflicted. At the bar our tortuous attempts at sign language for a beer were met with the stark information that they didn't accept Russian money. "I only vant sterling or dollars" was the cry at this point. I noticed a few furtive Libyans disappearing out of sight. A shady compromise was quickly reached though, before the situation got out of hand, and it was strawberry flavoured lager all round. If you didn't fancy that you could always try peach!

I was sharing a room with Ken McCluskey who sang with the Bluebells pop group. Remember their Number One chart hit 'Young at heart'? Teatime turned into a bit of a farce. We were offered Chicken Kiev, and with Kiev being just 66 miles from Chernobyl there was a loud request for the lights to be turned out "to see if it glows in the dark!" My cold squashed pie from Littlewoods was becoming more appetising by the minute!

A wedding was taking place in the next room and before the happy couple knew it they had about 60 extra guests, leaping about the dance floor high on strawberry and apricot lager! A 22 stone lover of Stella Artois from my local pub in Glasgow decided to tie a Celtic scarf rather tightly around the neck of the bride who proceeded to dance around with it on the entire evening. The groom, not to be outdone, took a liking to an Irish Tricolour and wore it as a cape!

Ken and myself decided to go out for a walk, unaware that there was a street curfew in force. After walking for about a mile we turned a corner and literally ran into a soldier standing to attention holding a gun in an upright position. The place was silent, dark and eerie and the soldier didn't move a muscle. Walking through Glasgow's Possilpark at 3.00am suddenly felt more appealing!

Seconds later a large black car which looked like an upmarket Lada drew up and the bloke in the passenger seat told us to get in, which we did, with no argument. The guy spoke very little English and all we blurted out was "Tourist, tourist."

Minutes later we were back outside our hotel, with us explaining why we were in Kiev, if it wasn't obvious already! He asked what we did in Scotland and what it was like living there. Ken explained he was a musician and, believe me, that saved the day. Our man in the vinyl car coat started to play an imaginary trumpet and it was obvious from his behaviour he was wanting to spend a bit of time in our company talking about music, much to our horror.

Thinking of ways to get out of the situation, I suggested that we got out of the car and Ken and myself would go to the room and fetch a bottle of whisky we had brought. "We have whisky for you my friend, we have whisky for you. It is in the room. We shall just go and get it for you. Will that be OK?" His eyes lit up and I was thinking "Please God, say yes you fat Russian B."

As he nodded, we started to head out of the car and just when we thought we'd done it, he grabbed Ken's arm. "You go and you stay here," he said. Ken's last words to me were, "Matt, make sure you come back, right." I will never forget the look of impending doom on his face. I met a couple of fans in the hotel and I was all a bit too stunned to let them know what was going on down in the car park, as they staggered around full of the peach and apricot lager.

Ken's first words on my return with the required cargo were: "What F'ing kept you?" "Relax," I said, "I've got the whisky and I brought him a Forfar bridie. Wait till he eats this!"

Ken and I spent the next hour there, which to be honest was quite pleasant. We spoke about music and whisky and he told us he was in the KGB and how he would love to come to Scotland (although we knew he would never have the opportunity to do so). And did he love that bridie! During all of this time his driver sat motionless in the driver's seat, not speaking a word. We shook hands and parted company, I suppose feeling relieved, and only slightly dazed.

The following day, Tuesday, myself and a couple of others (Ken was nowhere to be seen!) decided to walk into the centre of the city. What a dismal-looking place. On every corner fat 50-year-old women wearing wraparound garments were employed to brush leaves off the street. Everybody looked miserable. The place was bereft of colour, and all the cars looked the same. It could have been Larkhall in November really!

As we were walking down the street a couple of young locals sidled up beside us. "Please don't turn around, there are people following us (as if we didn't know!) "Can we show you around Kiev?" "For F's sake, he must be a tourist guide," said Tam. As we walked on further, it became obvious that they just wanted to meet us and say hello.

They looked in amazement at our Levi jeans and Nike trainers. They asked "Can we swop?" To be honest, I had no desire for their clothes, but at the same time I did feel sorry for them. When we shook off our guard we went into what resembled a coffee house. Basically, they wanted Western type clothing which they either would keep for themselves or sell on the very lucrative black market. The others and I decided that we would take them back to the hotel and see what we had that we could possibly give them.

They explained that the security guards would spot them and they would get picked up. I said, "Not if you shove on a Celtic scarf and baseball cap". This they did and our white-faced Russian pals were in seventh heaven.

That evening, which was to be our last night in town, was to be spent in the hotel lounge. You couldn't go out and try a few bars like you could in other cities in Europe. It struck me that I hadn't yet seen a Russian woman whom you would class as "attractive" in a western sense - until now!

In the lounge which held the 100 or so Celtic fans were three women. Two other Celts were already on the scene and for purposes of confidentiality I will refer to them only as Liam and Gerry, as they both had partners back home! Two of the girls' names I can remember, Natasha and Irena. The third slips me but she will make an appearance further on in this story.

Liam, Gerry and myself sat with the three Russian girls who spoke perfect English. The evening progressed, but with our large audience of fellow Celts in attendance it was proving a touch difficult under the circumstances to display 'yir true Glasgow charm'. However as my mother would say, these things were sent to try us, and try I did!

Let's be honest here: I was hoping to spend some time back in Natasha's flat, but perhaps that was not the way they did things in 'pre-glasnost' Russia. It had been made clear earlier that the girls would not be allowed up to our room (only for the purpose of sampling our duty free of course!) as the security hadn't taken their eyes off us all evening. As it turned out, me and Liam got invited back to Natasha's flat, which we were assured was only 2 minutes away. Now you might find this hard to believe, but as we were about to enter the taxi an older gentleman from our crowd who was about 68 years old suddenly appeared and pushed Gerry out of the way and sped off in the taxi alone with the girl with no name!

Poor Gerry went back into the bar with a fair number of guys doing their best not to laugh. The feeling he had must be similar to that of a footballer who is about to climb the steps to receive the trophy, only to be told he is dreaming and the other team have in fact won his prize.

Meanwhile, Natasha, Irena, Liam and myself all headed off into the deserted Kiev night. This journey which was meant to last two minutes was now taking 20 and for the second time in 24 hours I was fearing for my safety. After 30 minutes I was honestly wishing we hadn't taken up Natasha's offer.

The flat, though, was better than I thought it would be. Compact, with a wooden varnished floor, no carpets, but warm with a central heating system coming up through the floor. I noticed a picture in a cabinet which looked like the Virgin Mary but was slightly different. I asked Natasha who it was and she made moves to cover it by standing in front of it and ushering me into the kitchen.

We were offered some sort of liquor and being like any man I was more interested in trying to assess this bizarre situation. I tasted the drink which was disgusting but being in the lap of the gods I didn't want to offend. At an opportune moment the drink hit the plant pot behind me. The poor plant probably died instantly!

The following morning I was awakened by the sound of heavy banging on the door. Natasha said, "Lie still, it may be soldiers." Lie still, I thought I was having an attack of rigor mortis! My heart was beating like a drum as I waited for whoever to burst through the door. Whoever it was went away, but by this time I was emotionally wasted. East had tasted West the previous night, but there was no chance of it happening again in the morning!

Natasha and I had arranged to meet that lunchtime. All I could think of was getting back to the Hotel Intourist. As we left the flat alone Natasha said it would be too dangerous for us to be seen together.

Safely back at the hotel I bumped into Tony McGuinness, who had something to do with the Celtic Boys Club. I was in a bedraggled state and looked like I had just been dragged through a hedge backwards. McGuinness said to me, "Is it you who runs Paul McStay's fan club?" I nodded, "Yes." He took another look at me and said, "I was going to enrol my niece in it. I don't think I'll bother now!"

At lunchtime Natasha and I went for a walk and she asked if she could listen to my Sony Walkman which was playing a Beatles tape. I can vividly remember the track being 'The Long and Winding Road'. I turned to her and she was crying her eyes out. Why do men say the most blindingly bland things at moments of emotional stress such as this? "Is there something wrong?" I ventured. We stopped and she just let go with everything. Now remember I am a normal guy from Glasgow over to watch his team playing a game of football. This is what she told me, almost word for word.

She worked for the Intelligence Service (the KGB) and had

done so for over six years. She had fallen in love with a West German doctor who wrote to her constantly and wanted her to join him in the West. But working in such a sensitive job she had no chance of getting out of the country. She had met him in much the same way she had met me. Natasha and the other two girls were told to go into the Hotel and mix with the Western tourists and listen to what was being said. Not that you would learn much from 100 football fans only interested in getting blitzed on apricot lager!

I ended up giving her the Sony Walkman, £30 and my address. Don't ask me why. The game now seemed immaterial and my head was buzzing!

A few of us headed for the team hotel where the players were milling about outside.

Back in Glasgow Arthur Haggerty, a truly remarkable character, had started a zany Celtic Supporters Club called the 'Wullie Malloys'. His strategy was if you saw a famous person anywhere, then you gave him a plastic 'Wullie' card. This made him a member whether he wanted to join or not.

The only famous person I know who actually agreed to be on the committee was Celtic's Paul McStay, he was the President. Graeme Souness, the Rangers manager at the time, was sent a card and the accompanying letter which informed him: "If you don't reply within seven days then you automatically become Honorary Leader of the Opposition." This he duly became. The same happened when I met Lord McCluskey, the High Court judge and a big Celtic man, at the Roy Aitken Testimonial Dinner in Glasgow's Albany Hotel in 1988.

Outside the Celtic team hotel in Kiev there was this rather important looking man, surrounded by bodyguards who had been visiting the Celtic party. I thrust a 'Wullie' card into his hand and he quickly pushed it into his pocket. The committee was now formed! We never did find out the Russian Official's name. I said to Arthur that perhaps he was the Minister for Sport, or something like that. Arthur knew of a Russian poet called Lev Mayakovsky and so that now became his name!

Paul McStay was President, Graeme Souness was

Honorary Leader of the Opposition, Lord McCluskey was our legal adviser and Lev Mayakovsky was the Overseas Minister for Sport. Arthur was the Chairman and I was the PR Officer.

The game.

The stadium was huge and held 107,000 that night. We were barely seated when along came soldiers in big coats holding cameras. They systematically went along in a line and photographed all of the Scottish fans as they watched the game, many of them unaware of what was going on. Celtic lost the game 3-1 with Mark McGhee, who got the man-of-the-match award, scoring for us. I recall it was 2-1 to Kiev with seconds remaining and Celtic pressing for the second goal that would put us through on the away goals rule. Despite an impressive display against a team who were then expected to go all the way it was yet another glorious failure for Celtic as the Russians added their third with almost the last kick of the ball.

As we left the stadium I witnessed a situation which, from time to time, flashes back into my mind. On our way back to the airport our bus stopped at traffic lights. Stopped next to us, and going in the opposite direction, was a bus crammed with very young Russian soldiers. They were staring into our bus, their faces painting a picture of utter bleakness and hopelessness. We just stared back, motionless. I remember catching one guy's eye and we both just looked at each other for about 20 seconds and the bus moved off. As it did I raised my hand to wave and he did the same. I wondered what he was thinking and he probably wished he was going where we were going.

To cap this incredible trip off I noticed ice on the inside rim of the Aeroflot plane's window! Honestly, I was past caring, I just wanted to sleep. I do remember just before I went to sleep Gerry McNee (the 'Sunday Mail' columnist) walking round all the fans on the aircraft and offering them a shot of whisky - I seriously doubt if he could bring himself to do the same now.

At this time I was staying with my mother in Mosspark while my divorce proceedings progressed. Around three weeks after Kiev an Airmail letter from Russia arrived for me. "It's got funny writing on it and lipstick kisses on the back," my mother shouted, suspiciously. Natasha had written. Another followed about a month later.

I never wrote back, perhaps I should have but then again I was not her West German doctor.

Smears, Lies and Audio Tapes

I was depressed that I had to get involved in the fight for Celtic's soul. It should never ever have come to that. But what depressed me more was the dirty tactics of some people who claimed to always have Celtic's best interests at heart. Our side were not prepared to enter into a smear campaign and I didn't think anyone in the opposite camp would attempt anything like that either. How wrong I was.

I am not trying to portray myself as a saint. I have had more than my fair share of scrapes. Being brought up in Govan and Drumoyne, and progressing into Pollok, I could hardly avoid some situations. The rules were pretty simple. Apply those wing mirrors and watch your back at all times!

One thing, though, that you were never taught as you ran up and down Kempsthorn Road was malicious intent.

I have always been of the opinion that if you love something then you must be prepared to fight for it. The Celtic situation was simple. Celtic reflected my aspirations, my ethics, my principles, my whole way of life. And I began to see it crumbling and being destroyed before my eyes. Therefore I had no choice but to get involved.

When dealing with such an emotive subject as Celtic, you are bound to step on a few toes. Some of the reactions I encountered were along the lines of "He's a smart ass, who does he think he is? Talking on the TV, telling us Celtic have problems." Yes I got plenty of that. Often in Glasgow if you stick your head above the parapet there will be plenty of punters ready to take it off, whether they agree with what you are saying or not.

Being thrust into the public's glare after remaining fairly anonymous for most of your life certainly has it's drawbacks. One minute you're standing in the Horseshoe Bar in Glasgow having a pint and the next minute someone's pointing at you and telling his pal in stage whispers "There's that tosser who was on the telly last night!" Maybe it comes with the territory, but it still takes a bit of getting used to. Often the only thing that keeps you going is the firm belief that you are doing the right thing and that others, whose opinions you value and respect, think the same as you do.

One of the first smears I encountered was "McGlone prints Rangers T-Shirts". This was designed to turn people against you and to sow the seeds of doubt in your mind and, ultimately, to damage your credibility as a genuine Celtic supporter.

I recall watching Celtic at Pittodrie in the last game of the season in May 1994. I was spotted in the crowd by a group of people who had obviously swallowed the "Rangers T-shirt" line.

The abuse I took towards the end of the first half and during half-time was incredible. "You don't know this guy. I know him. I'll tell you about his past. He's an opportunist. He's just in this to make money out of Celtic!" He continued in this vein; that I was printing Rangers shirts and was some sort of Fagan character employing kids to sell the fanzine I edited, inferring that they were so young they didn't have a clue what they were selling.

I will answer both of these allegations forthwith. But I want to mention something more important. With me at Pittodrie was my girlfriend at the time Elaine who also had to endure all of this. Also in the company was my friend on the 'Celts For Change' committee Colin Duncan. Elaine suffered from multiple sclerosis and all of this was making her upset and unwell. So much so that she was on the verge of collapsing. Yes all of this coming from a guy who wore the same colour of wool around his neck as me!

Supporters stood about in astonishment as the verbal attack continued. At this point Elaine was standing up and sitting down and generally becoming disorientated. I put my arms around her to support her and the guy shouted "Look at him hugging his burd for comfort!" I am not a violent person, but at this point I could feel the red mist descending and I began to make my way over the seats in his direction. Thankfully other decent supporters began to get involved and moved into the guy and his mates and sorted the situation out.

I later found out the name of this individual who had given us so much grief that day and could easily print his name here. But I don't intend to. I would rather Elaine and I received an apology over the incident.

Elaine had a bit of an attack with her illness and she didn't feel like travelling back to Glasgow, so we booked into a hotel. She was unfit to travel until the Monday, the same day we were meant to be travelling to Manchester to watch Celtic and Manchester United in the Mark Hughes Testimonial. But she was too shattered by the events.

As I was going into Old Trafford I was approached by a guy called Jim Cameron, who was one of the lads who helped sort the situation out at Aberdeen two days earlier. I will always be grateful to him and others for their help that day. We have enjoyed a few beers since that afternoon.

With regard to the T-shirt smear. In the late 1980s a guy whom I had worked with in the printing industry many years earlier came into partnership with me and we opened a T-shirt business in Glasgow's South Side. When Celtic won the double in 1988 and the Scottish Cup in 1989 we had T-shirts on the streets with the score printed on them before 5.15pm. I was at both games but he had no interest in Celtic and so both he and the apprentice listened to the game on the radio, awaiting the score to print on the shirt.

The fact that he had no interest in Celtic meant he wasn't averse to printing Rangers T-Shirts if a customer required them. He did own half the business! Do we only sell our cars or our houses to Celtic fans? Do we all work only for Celtic supporters? Is it only Rangers fans who work in the Adidas factory making Rangers shirts? Was I expected to dictate to my business partner who was not a Celtic fan, and who had money invested in the business, that he only printed Celtic gear?

On the question of wee boys selling the fanzine. Yes they did. My two sons were earning pocket money for their holidays and they loved every minute of it, out there on the street with the big guys selling the fanzine and shouting, "Once A Tim Always A Tim." Celtic supporters out there having fun and making money at the same time for their efforts.

Potentially the most damaging and serious line of cheap smears was when an individual called Gerry McSherry was furnished with private and confidential information regarding my finances and also some debts I may have accumulated over the years. Apparently if you owe money to a bank or finance company then a search of your finances can be obtained through a data bank.

McSherry phoned me and told me he had a file regarding my personal finances which had been sent to him by a certain individual whom I will name further on, and that he was sending this information around the press and TV and anyone who would listen to him. This was an attempt to defame me personally and derail the 'Celts For Change' campaign which was being run by honest, working-class Celtic supporters, only interested in seeing their Club run properly. Who says it's only a game of football? My first thoughts were, "Who is behind this?" This was not some guy feeding off street rumours. This was a clear attempt at something a bit more sinister. This time I did intend to take it personally. McSherry was obviously being used by someone (a bit smarter than himself) to do their dirty work.

I rang McSherry back and demanded he told me who was behind this. He told me to go away and that we ('Celts For Change') would be defeated soon and then hung up. My next approach 15 minutes later was that if he didn't tell me who was behind this smear I would take legal action and take a writ out against him. His reply was "Post it, I'll paper my wall with it."

I made my mind up then that he should tell me. So I gave it half an hour and phoned him back and quietly explained to him that although he backed the Board he was clearly being used and that if the people behind it had any guts then they would do it themselves. This at last appeared to make an impression on his brain. "Naebody uses me" he said "The Kellys and Whites are Celtic people. You and your gang are just thugs. We will defeat you, nae danger. Your guys came up to my garden and kicked down my 40 foot fence. At this point I wasn't sure whether to laugh or humour him. One minute it was smear campaigns involving him and A.N. Other, the next it was his garden fence being uprooted. I couldn't even tell you if he lived in a flat or a mansion. I quietly told him that if he didn't tell me who was using him and attempting to set me up then I would print this entire chapter in the fanzine. "You wouldn't," he said. "Don't you worry" I replied.

He doubted me, but I was perfectly serious and he knew it.

"OK," he said. "All I can tell you is that it is a relation to a member of the current Celtic Board." Now you can imagine how I felt at this point. McSherry was down and I was counting to 10. On the seventh phone call McSherry caved in and blurted out: "His name is John Fulton and he is Kevin Kelly's son in law."

I immediately went to my solicitor's office. This is the exact text of the next conversation McSherry and myself had. If he doubts any of it I will take great pleasure in proving it to him or Fulton, word for word.

11/1/94: Conversation between Matt McGlone and Gerry McSherry at approximately 10.45am

MM: "Gerry? How are you? It's Matt."

GM: "I was on to Michael Kelly this morning and I've told him that I've been set up and I don't like it one little bit and I'm taking nothing more to do with Fulton. I've been used here, Matt and I don't like it. I don't like it and you don't like it and that's why I apologised to you this morning."

MM: "Well, I'll tell you what it was. I've been thinking about it as well, I mean, we're all in this for Celtic. Nobody wants any dirt going anywhere, untruths or anything. I'm prepared to forget all about the whole thing but what I want you to do to keep the whole thing above board and clear is for you to send me a letter just saying where you heard the information on the £30,000. I am not worried about any of the other things but..."

GM: "Matt, that's common knowledge that £30,000, that's why I know."

MM: "Yes, I know, but a lot of people have been phoning me up, the press, all the rest-of it. It's in the 'Record' today - Alex Cameron phoned me up. What I want you to do is send me a letter just for the record I want it in writing, really, Gerry..."

GM: "What difference does it make, Matt? I've told you."

MM: "I know you've told me... because these people are trying to push it."

GM: "I know, and I want to distance myself from it. I don't want to be involved any more."

MM: "Right, OK, I just want to tie bits up neatly, but we'll leave it at that then, OK...I won't push it any further. Alex Cameron phoned me up last night and said: I heard you've got £30,000... and I said it was utter rubbish...and that was what the comment was in the paper. The thing is ridiculous but obviously he didn't get it from you, he got it from some other source."

GM: "That's what it is...it's a rumour that's been going around for a while, you know, it wasn't just John Fulton that told me that, there are others as well."

MM: "Other people?"

GM: "I'll tell you why..."

MM: "Other people told you that?... Did other people tell you that?"

GM: "People who phoned me up, aye. What they say is,

can you tell me, have you heard the rumour about Matt McGlone being given £30,000 by…in fact, it wasn't Dempsey it was McCann, right? There were some who said it was Dempsey, but the point is Matt, I know that me and you disagree, right, in the best way to handle the Celtic thing, right, as I say, the dirty tricks stuff I'm not interested in because I believe that Celtic can defeat you, right, but by legitimate means, through board meetings and all the rest of it and there is no need to resort to it and that's why I'm so angry with Fulton for trying to drag me into the s…, right. I believe that we can defeat you Matt and by legitimate means…"

MM: "Aye, we'll always disagree on that so that's irrelevant…"

GM: "…You agree, but, I feel an injustice has been done to you Matt."

MM: "Oh there has been an injustice done, yes, 'cause that's why I was so angry yesterday."

GM: "Oh, I know, and you've a right to be angry. I was talking to, what do you call him, I'm just going to George McKechnie, the editor of the Evening Times, right. Now he wasn't in, and his secretary, I've told her that I've been set up and I don't like it one little bit. Hopefully it'll be sorted out, I'm determined. I'm going to continue to do what I can to enable this to be sorted and I hope I never meet the guy. As I say I've never met any of them Matt. Kelly's never phoned me. None of them phone me. I phone them…."

MM: "But you were talking to Michael on Sunday."

GM: "I was talking to him on Sunday, as I say. I phoned him on Sunday and I told him about the allegations and I told him this guy who was wanting to set up a group to combat yourself, right. And I told him I wasn't interested in that. I told you about the story in the News of the World that you are talking about Matt. That was a load of mince."

MM: "Och well, best just leaving it Gerry and forget the whole thing."

GM: "Aye well I'm not going to bring you into it any further. Your name will be used obviously, but I'm determined to nail Fulton because this sort of stuff discredits everybody connected with the Club, likes of yourself especially, you know the malicious stuff and all the rest of it, and it brings discredit to the Club and it discredits myself and, as I say, I put the blame firmly and squarely on Fulton. That he tried it and I was a fool to fall for it."

MM: "Right, OK, fair enough then, Gerry. Nice speaking to you."

GM: "OK, Matt, Cheers."

MM: "See you, bye bye."

I met John Fulton on two occasions afterwards with Colin Duncan, fellow committee member of 'Celts For Change'. Once at Celtic Park on March 30th, 1994 when he sheepishly approached both of us and attempted to apologise for his involvement with Gerry McSherry. We again met outside Old Trafford on May 16th, 1994 at the Mark Hughes testimonial match. Again he said he was sorry. I met him on my own at a petrol station in Glasgow about a month after this and he repeated his apology and suggested lunch.

Another smear story was that 'Celts For Change' had received £30,000 from either Brian Dempsey or Fergus McCann to run their campaign. Fergus was either in Arizona or Canada and as I didn't have much contact with him I turned to Brian and asked him to nail these smears.

We were the ones who still had to go about our business on the streets of Glasgow, and I and the other four in the 'CFC' committee wanted Brian to sort this rubbish out and stop whoever was spreading the untruths. To be fair to Dempsey he had 100 other more important matters to sort out with regard to attempting to remove the real problems at Celtic Park, namely the jokers on the Board!

Had these people got away with it they would have been quite prepared to marginalise me by telling the world tawdry and nasty innuendo about things that had nothing to do with them.

Each and every one of them are pathetic individuals. McSherry never crosses his door to watch Celtic but Fulton still swans about inside Parkhead and attempts a wee nod in my direction every so often.

Eye to Eye with Michael Kelly

It was one of those close-season Saturday afternoons. No football and at a loose end. It was a brilliantly sunny day for a change and I decided to take my daughter Kirsty for a walk. At the time in summer 1981 she was 2 years old. At this point in my life I was married to Jackie, the mother of my three children, and we lived in Leven Street, Pollokshields, Glasgow.

Around the corner in Kenmure Street was a small park. As we approached the park I noticed a reasonable crowd had gathered and as we reached the gates my enquires led me to believe that the Lord Provost of Glasgow was in attendance. That would be Michael Kelly thought I. He was opening some kind of Fete. I thought to myself that I would like to meet this guy.

When the moment was right I stepped forward and offered my outstretched hand to him. "Nice to meet you Mr Kelly." He shook my hand warmly and said "Thank you," nodding at the same time. I will be perfectly honest here, I was well chuffed, I had met a guy who was well-respected, he was the Lord Provost of Glasgow, and somewhere down the line I knew he had a connection with the Celtic.

There was also another very good reason why I wanted to shake his hand. He was a Catholic from Glasgow who had done well for himself in this sectarian city of ours, and I reckoned he must have worked pretty hard to get into this position particularly with his name and his Celtic background. Being brought up in Glasgow you realised very quickly that with an Irish Catholic name you would face some difficulties getting on and applying for most jobs around Glasgow.

Now around that time my mother Mary Theresa worked for a Boston Company called Trans National Travel. Although she was in the twilight of her working life she was still very sprightly and active. One of her tasks was to meet the tourists when they arrived from the USA and welcome them to the Holiday Inn in Glasgow.

Another duty she had was to take the tourists to the City Chambers Building in George Square to meet Michael Kelly the Lord Provost. Mary Theresa's official quote is: "I was very happy with him and I respected Michael. He was also very good with the tourists." Can't say fairer than that can you?

That was about it with Michael until May 1990 when he was co-opted onto the Celtic Board along with a guy I had never heard of called Brian Dempsey. At that time I thought "Brilliant, two new Celtic Directors!" This was about the first time I could recollect any significant changes on the Celtic Board, and I was obviously pleased.

There was a photograph taken at the time and it shows Kelly and Dempsey holding a large cake together, with Michael's arm resting on Brian's shoulder. The wording on the cake said "Celtic's Smiles Better." I'll bet neither of them have that picture on their mantelpiece at home any more!

Things at Parkhead were fairly quiet from May until October that year and then Bang! Dempsey was unceremoniously kicked off the Celtic Board three days before the Skol Cup Final.

It became clear via the press and certain Celtic contacts that this action had been engineered by Chris White and Michael Kelly, the man whom I had much respect for. Brian, it seemed, had been wronged and stabbed in the back by these

First Communion
St. Constantines, Govan 1961.

On holiday 1964 with Mary & Dad.
(Cool car, shame about the jumper!)

First 'Celts For Change' Rally!
Morecambe 1964.

On the Hallowed Turf in
The Estadio Nacional, Lisbon.

The Mini McGlones
(LtoR) Nicholas, Kirsty & Gary.

From Russia with love. With Natasha in Kiev.

Outside Shettleston Town Hall with Brian Dempsey, February '91.

Every Bhoy's dream. Back at Celtic Park on the night with the Scottish Cup, 27th May, 1995.

Tommy Carberry owner of Bairds Celtic Bar in Glasgow's Calton.
(With Willie O'Neill's European Cup Medal).

Me and Davie with Jimmie O'Neil of Scottish rock group, The Silencers in the New Paradise.

In the beginning.

These pictures illustrate how the campaign grew in size, heralding the downfall of the old regime.

The end of the road.

The Rebels have won. Celebrations outside Celtic Park as news of the takeover reaches the faithful.

The rebel alliance with Dominic Keane & Celtic saviour Fergus McCann, under the watchful gaze of big Jock.

Billy Smith and myself with Billy (Hail Caesar!) McNeill.

(Right) With the Cup no Rangers player will ever hold!

Showing a young Paul McStay how to pose for team photo's!

Giving Tommy Burns a few pointers. Advice he would draw upon in future years. Not!

HAPPY DAYS ARE HERE AGAIN!

The 'Celts For Change' committee are guests of the club for the first home game after the takeover, 19th March 1994.

(L to R) Brendan Sweeney, Colin Duncan, Myself, David Cunningham & John Thompson.

two, and apparently the other Board members didn't know anything about Kelly and White's intention until minutes before it happened, at the Club's AGM.

The Celtic support were incensed at this decision, and it is at this point where I think the real split began between the support and the Board.

Now, if you were to believe Kelly's bizarre account of Dempsey's removal in his book published last year, which goes into tedious detail about shady land deals and upholding Celtic's honour, then you would have expected, surely, Kelly to have gone public with it. If the world and his granny are against you then you are naturally going to want to set the record straight, at least to avert the mounting criticism flying in your direction. That would make sense would it not? And to this day that is why I am not convinced by the reason Michael Kelly gave four years later. What I have discovered through all of the Celtic tribulations is that some people just don't come clean about certain situations. This happens on both sides of the fence. It's all deflection, shadow boxing, and mind chess.

In November of 1990 I became Editor of the Celtic fanzine 'Once a Tim, Always a Tim'. For some reason various people reckoned that was a pretty naff name for a fanzine. I however, thought it was pretty apt. After all it was a street magazine, and the street name for a Celtic fan was a Tim.

In November, 1990 I attended the Glasgow University Celtic Supporters Club 20th Anniversary Night along with a dozen or so friends. Sean Fallon, who was big Jock's assistant during the 1960s and 70s, was guest of honour. The speeches were spiritual in a Celtic sense and a great evening was in progress as we dined and wined to excess. Even at my age I was still in awe of people like Sean Fallon simply because he was part of something which meant a great deal to me, and what these people had achieved was far beyond what I was ever capable of achieving for Celtic.

Anyway, full of the evening frolics I headed down to the gents. Standing there, minding my own business as it were, I noticed a figure whom I knew as David Low. I had seen him on television talking about Celtic's troubles and knew he was in the rebel camp, i.e., involved with Brian Dempsey's group.

Only days earlier I had heard a whisper that he was involved in offering Celtic shareholders good money for their shares which had an unknown present value and had either been handed down through generations or had cost £1 each. Now it must be remembered that at this point in Celtic history the changing hands of shares was virtually unknown or was very rare. Business was usually only done amongst certain families.

I looked over in Low's direction as I washed my hands and said to him "Excuse me, are you David Low?"

"That's right," he replied.

"My name's Matt McGlone, I'm the Editor of "Once A Tim"."

"Hi, how are you?" came his reply.

"I've heard that you have been buying up Celtic shares on behalf of certain people, is that true?"

At this point Low's shoes almost changed from normal brogues to wet look brogues! "Where did you hear that?" he asked.

"I can't remember, but is it true? Because I'm going to print it in the fanzine." Low looked a bit perplexed and said "The Celtic Board don't even know about this. Keep it to yourself just now. Here's my phone number. Phone me tomorrow and I'll let you know what's going on."

From around about that time we became fellow rebels in the fight against the Celtic Board. In fact, knowing what I know now, I can safely say that there would have been no takeover of the Celtic Board in March 1994 had it not been for Low's involvement.

Although money men eventually came in, the tactics for purchasing shares were Low's brainchild.

It could be suggested that the Board would inevitably have gone. But my answer to that is, surely it is better to have a structured takeover, rather than have a great club like Celtic go into liquidation and then be prey to any speculator intent on making a fast buck. It was the smart people who recognised this fact.

The fanzine had made quite a name for itself and had produced around 12 issues up until November 1992. It wasn't a rabble. It was well-structured and had a good mix of serious points with plenty of satirical humour thrown in alongside crosswords and cartoons. The Board themselves had their own cartoon called 'The Board Stiffs'! They were ridiculed at every opportunity in print and cartoon form.

In just about every issue they got it in the neck, and this helped keep the pressure on.

Thursday, November 20th, 1992 is a day I won't forget in a hurry. Pushing the button on my flashing answering machine I was astonished to hear Michael Kelly's voice. I thought it was a spoof but at the back of my mind I knew it wasn't. Why would this man, who had become my opponent, want to speak to me? If I was Michael Kelly, Matt McGlone would be the last person whom I would want to engage in conversation.

His opening gambit was: "Hello Matt, it's Michael Kelly. I wonder if you could give me a call. I have an interesting proposition for you."

I couldn't work it out at all, but I was returning his call all the same. When I did so I asked him what he wanted. He said he didn't want to discuss it on the phone and could we meet quite soon. We arranged to meet the following day at 12 noon.

Now, I will be perfectly honest with you. I didn't trust the guy at all. Rightly or wrongly there was an instinct telling me to be careful and to be aware of the possibility of some kind of set-up. With this in mind I decided to put a tape in my top pocket so that if he said anything other than what was discussed then I could easily prove otherwise.

At about 11.55am I entered the building he ran his PR Company from in Glasgow's Bothwell Street. As I travelled up on the lift I checked my watch as the tape would click off in exactly one hour and I didn't want to be sitting there engaged in conversation and all of a sudden he hears the obvious click of the tape.

As I entered his office I was greeted by a chap with a famous Celtic name, John Thompson. I was shown into Kelly's office and he followed about a minute later. A faint smile came from Kelly followed by a fairly weak handshake, unlike the one I got from him 11 years earlier.

My bum had hardly hit the seat when Kelly said, "Right let's pass the buck right away. David Smith wants to do this. No matter what you think of the Celtic Board I'm sure you agree that the media coverage we get is absolutely horrendous."

Now I'm sitting there thinking that this guy is completely oblivious to the very fact that the way he and others are running our Club is in fact the very reason the headlines are so bad.

I was quickly alerted to his complete lack of understanding of what was happening in the real world. That he either refused to accept he and the others were not respected at all amongst the majority of the paying customers, or he was so detached from the reality of the problem he probably thought in his own wee innocent mind that he was doing his best for the Club, and that all of this resentment would blow over.

As a person I didn't dislike him. I disliked his audacity and his manner, and his disregard for the fact that there were supporters out there who had a different point of view from him. I always got the feeling that he regarded Celtic, our Club, as his own wee private club. His to keep open, or to close down, and that we, the supporters, were mere peripherals.

In his book he said of me: "I answered every question he had about the current situation, assuming him to be a genuine Celtic supporter."

Here we have a classic example of his complete lack of understanding of anyone who disagreed with his ideas for Celtic. In his mind you are not a genuine Celtic fan if you don't go along with his way of thinking.

I couldn't take offence at that remark, not from him anyway.

He rambled on about how the Club couldn't get back at the media in the way the fans would like them to. "So David

Smith had this wonderful idea that in the Christmas edition of 'The Celtic View' the fanzine guys get the four inside pages and do to the media what you do to Celtic."

How could he be so blind to the fact that the people who didn't agree with his running of our Club would in fact not want to work for him. And more importantly carry out his dirty work. The fanzine's attitude was to support Celtic and fight for it's best interests. To this end we found ourselves at odds with the Board and found the machinations, double-dealing and back-stabbing that filled the media, an embarrassment.

But in order to rescue Celtic from this malaise we had to address the root problem. That was the Board.

I explained to Kelly that the fanzine had the opposite view to that of 'The Celtic View' and we were free to say what we wanted, and that working for him or his mates might not be the image we would want.

Most people would have understood that I was trying to be polite and just give up there. But Kelly persisted: "What we need is someone to write it in that style. I'm not saying that these pages are written by "Once A Tim"."

In effect we were to come into 'The Celtic View' under the cover of darkness and ghostwrite his four pages for free. That was also made clear as well. We were then to slip away in the middle of the night, as if nothing had happened and go back to criticising him and his wee gang of four who made up his immoral pact. Do you see what I mean about his complete lack of understanding? He just didn't care about anything other than his way of doing things.

Kelly went on: "The Club itself, we don't want to be seen to be involved in this." Now if I wasn't there to be used, then I had lost the plot! Earlier a cup of tea had been placed in front of me, but as I don't drink tea or coffee it more or less remained as it was. I glanced at my watch and the hour was only minutes away. As Kelly rambled on my main concern was how I was going to get out of his clutches so that he wouldn't hear the tape click off.

This was now not going to be possible so I came up with

the ingenious idea of tapping the tea cup with my spoon, like a drummer! So if the tape clicked off then he wouldn't be able to distinguish the sounds. I was trying hard to keep my face straight and I kept thinking of serious things like funerals. I remember looking at him, and he looking back at me as if I was enjoying his company, as I drummed away with my spoon. I couldn't think of enough funerals and almost lost it at one point but my worst thoughts kept my face straight!

I glanced at my watch and we were now at an hour and five minutes. The click had come and gone and even I hadn't noticed it. He, meanwhile, was oblivious to all of this and was still going on about his wee plot.

Why should the fanzine defend the Board when they are clearly defending their interests against those of the Club? Why should 'OAT' or anyone else form a buffer zone around the Board when what we wanted to do at the time was to get existing barriers out of the way and get right at them ourselves.

I went into Heraghtys Bar that night and told the lads about my lunch time escapade. Some of the comments were quite choice and I was offered several unrepeatable lines for Michael when I was to call him back on the Monday.

I phoned him first thing Monday morning and his opening line was "What's this about Peel Holdings?"

Peel Holdings was a company who I recollected apparently had first rights to the poisoned field at Cambuslang where Celtic had been telling everyone they were planning to build a new stadium for nothing.

"What about Peel Holdings?" I asked.

"I'm asking you what it is about" said Kelly.

"How do you mean?" I replied.

Whilst I thought I was on some kind of game show over the phone with him, he seemed to be getting more agitated as time went on and I still didn't have a clue what he was on about.

"No, no, no. It was a press enquiry today and they said that you were involved in it."

I then thought that perhaps I really was beginning to lose the plot and I asked him what this was all about and where it came from.

"I can't disclose my sources, but you'll probably read it in the paper today though."

Well almost three years later and I'm still waiting to read it in the paper, and find out what he was babbling on about.

Anyway it was time to give him the Nine o'clock News. "I've been thinking about what you said on Friday. The way I see it Michael is, basically, my stand is that the Celtic Board, including you, are not really representative of the supporters and you don't have the Club's best interests at heart. I don't think it is what I would want to be involved in."

"Even though you would be writing it anonymously?"

"We are the fanzine and you are 'The Celtic View' and I don't see any point in a marriage between the two." At last I was making an impression on him.

"You do have an editorial staff at 'The Celtic View' who can do what you are looking for?"

"Well, we'll probably do that," he replied. "It's got to be written, there's no doubt about that. It's just that you guys have developed a style of doing it."

"We get plenty of practice!" I replied.

"Okay, Matt, thanks for getting back so quickly. Goodbye." And that, as they say, was that.

The Evening Times got to hear about the story and I gave them my account of what happened. I had nothing to hide, After all I didn't phone him. He phoned me and his sneaky plot had backfired on him. On the day the story hit the front pages the 'Evening Times' gave Michael an early morning alarm call at 7am, in person, on his doorstep.

Considering Michael was a public relations man you may be forgiven for thinking he could possibly have handled this in a more professional manner. His attempt to use a fanzine editor, who never agreed with him anyway, to get at the press was at the least embarrassing, and verging on the ridiculous.

Later that day I was walking up Union Street in Glasgow, and the headline on the billboards screamed "Celtic in plot to smear the Times". I would have thought it more appropriate for it to have read "Kelly in plot to smear the Times". After all, how many people at Celtic Park, apart from Vice-Chairman David Smith, actually knew about his wee scam?

My main front-page comment was "'The Celtic View' is simply an organ for their own rantings. If the Celtic Board wish to do a hatchet job on anybody I am sure they are more than capable of carrying it out themselves."

Back in his office, near the end of our chat, Michael said he liked the fanzine and reached for his cheque book to give me a yearly subscription of £6.00. I was cringing with embarrassment and told him not to bother and that I would send it out to him. Needless to say I never did.

Looking at all of this in the cold light of day I suppose you could say that if I had been gullible enough, or even overawed by his presence, and if we had carried out his wishes, then we as an independent voice would have carried absolutely no credibility in our fight to defeat the Board. That's why it was important to believe in what we were doing, and to believe that what we were engaged in was right. Smarter people use this type of tactic against what they consider weaker or less influential folk, hoping they will cave in, in their presence.

The Press

There was one particular episode where I was slightly duped, and the reason for this was because I took a man at face value, and trusted him. That man was Gerry McNee. This is where I made a mistake. McNee called me and asked me if he could hear the tape of my conversation with Michael Kelly. I was a bit hesitant as this was not the reason the recording had been made. It was made to make sure that I was not being set up by Kelly. In hindsight I should have said no to McNee. He was on the rebels' side, but not for the reasons I thought at the time. I thought, foolishly enough, that my aims for Celtic and the removal of the Board were the same as his. How wrong can you be.

McNee was in touch now and again during the campaign, and he was fed plenty of information by a lot of people. From what McNee has since told me, I now suspect he had a dislike of Michael Kelly. I didn't suspect this then, but by the time I realised it I had already allowed him to hear and copy the tape. This was some months after Kelly's plot had been exposed and therefore the relevance of its contents was somewhat diminished.

We had met in his tiny office at Scottish Television in Glasgow. Talk about nice. Here he was chirpy and cheery. You know your long-lost-pal sketch. I had no sooner sat down when he produced a small micro-cassette with a connecting wire to plug into mine.

I said to him that I didn't want him to make a copy. It was there for him to listen to it, as we both had a common ground in as much that we both wanted Kelly and the others out of Celtic Park. He categorically assured me that he would never use it. Some months later I was reading his column in the Scottish Daily Express and he made reference to a tape. I believed he had deceived me and I was raging.

I phoned him at home and told him what I thought of him. He attempted to laugh it off and said that he hadn't mentioned the director in person, but the reference was so obvious you would have had to have been a complete idiot not to put two and two together. I felt I couldn't trust him any more. Lesson learnt.

The night before the boycott game against Kilmarnock on February 25th, 1994 I was on BBC Sportscene talking about Celtic's plan to sell a minority of shares to the support. The Board claimed to have got involved with a bank which traded under the name of Gefinor.

It had been snowing all evening and it looked as though all of our best-laid plans for the following day were about to be avalanched. My plan after leaving the BBC was to go out with my friend Cathy once she had finished work at a Glasgow Hospital. Minutes before I was about to leave the phone rang. It was McNee. He jokingly pretended to be an angry fan who wanted the Board out.

At the end of his 'Rory Bremner' sketch he said "Fancy a drink. I have a couple of things to tell you." Half an hour later Cathy and I met him in Heraghtys Bar. He rambled on about how he did this, that and the next thing. How he had told this person where to go, and how he had put that person right. Cathy was none too impressed with his manner. Two drinks later and we were off at Plumpton back to her cosy wee flat.

McNee and myself had no further contact until October

14th, 1994 when he phoned me at home. He was telling me he had just picked up his copy of 'The Celtic View'. He was reading my column and asked me how I could agree with the Club's decision to sell a small number of tickets in a one-off situation in a package of 3 tickets, with the cheapest deal for 3 games being £25.00. That worked out at £8.33 per match, and it guaranteed the fan a ticket for the game everyone wanted to see, the Rangers game.

I explained to him that if you followed your team then it was a good deal, especially due to the fact that you were guaranteed a ticket for the Rangers game. This was only three games, remember, and over 18,000 supporters had paid up front for the entire season. I also mentioned in my article that "Sympathy, of course, must go to the genuine fans who are unemployed and will find it difficult to come up with £25.00 in a oner. Perhaps for the future a scheme could be devised whereupon unemployed fans who, understandably, cannot afford to buy season tickets or packages such as this, could perhaps have some kind of instalment card, which would enable them to pay it up." Here he was criticising the fact that fans who hadn't invested in buying a season ticket, unlike 18,000 others who had, were simply being offered a package which would enable them to watch three games for £25.00. It's called marketing, and at £8.33 to watch Celtic and Rangers you could hardly call it a rip-off.

I asked him if he was phoning for a comment for his Sunday Mail column. "No, no, I have already written my piece for this week."

I asked him why he continued to advise Celtic to remove the Irish Tricolour and why, in his own words, we should "Bin the bigotry and stop singing 'The Fields of Athenry'".

"What's it to do with football?" he replied.

"Well Celtic supporters are more of a culture, and in my opinion this is a cultural folk song about the Irish famine, a country where many thousands of Celtic supporters hail from."

"It is not a song riddled with hatred like many songs sung by Rangers supporters, i.e., "We're up to our knees in Fenian blood. Surrender or you'll die". McNee should perhaps preserve his rantings for songs like that.

Later on Rangers told their current season ticket holders that to guarantee their seat they would have to cough up another £399.00. Now you would think that surely this would be something for McNee to sink his teeth into. But no, all we got was silence. Can you imagine the headlines if we came up with such a scheme?

Two days after I spoke to him on the phone, his column appeared in the Sunday Mail. In it he was criticising Celtic's £8.33 offer. Of me he said: "We had the sickening sight of a former fanzine editor, who now takes the Club coin, backing this deal." I offered to debate this matter with him, live on TV, but he never took me up on this.

The difference is, I will back my Club to the hilt when they are right. I have stuck my neck out on a regular basis to point out the rights and wrongs at Celtic. I don't duck the issue, and I care about what I write and the consequences of that.

It was good of McNee to be so observant and notice that Celtic do pay me for my time in writing three-quarters of a page for the Club newspaper. I will also point out to him that I earn less writing in 'The Celtic View' than I ever did with the fanzine.

McNee on the other hand, must have been hoping that the carry-on with the Celtic Board could have lasted much longer. Months, even years. He could then have made so much more of it, as our Club slipped further and further towards a humiliating liquidation. What stuck out a mile about McNee was that, when the takeover was complete the new owners should have been given time to turn around an out-of-control juggernaut of debt, and find their feet. This he didn't do.

The job that Fergus McCann and his directors were faced with was unbelievable. Pay off other people's debts, demolish a crumbling stadium, plan and build a 21st century football stadium, employ a new management team to look after the side, plan a share issue (which was a fantastic success) create a structure for a solid future, and deal with a thousand other smaller problems which were inherited from the incompetents on the previous Board.

When the magnificent new north stand was erected McNee's comment was, as he sat in it: "You can see Ibrox from here!"

When the Club was taken over the fanzine was put to sleep. It was very anti the previous Board, and they had now gone. To carry on with the publication and criticise the new owners when they had so much work to do would have been hypocritical. We knew when to stop. It was time to lift the Club up from the pavement and encourage the new administration.

If the day ever comes and I am censored for telling the truth, then that is the day I will walk out of Celtic Park. Of that you can have no doubt. So far I have been able to write the situation as a fan would see it and how we would discuss it amongst ourselves. It has not all been plain sailing with the editor Andrew Smith, we have had our 'run-ins' on several occasions. Andrew printed the diatribe of the old Board, therefore our opinions were bound to clash! So long a he does not interfere with my articles I have no problem working for 'The Celtic View'. After all I was brought in to give an alternative view!

As far as Michael is concerned I must admit he was right once. In his book he says he made a "major mistake" in meeting me, as his wee plan backfired on him. Yes, on this occasion he was spot on. Michael's blurred vision of Celtic was because his family had shares in the Club and his predecessors were in at the beginning. This meant it always had to be that way. Perhaps that would have been the case if he had attempted to safeguard it's welfare. Nobody then would have wanted him or his chums out, and that is exactly where Michael slipped up.

Too many people emotionally depend on Celtic and all that it stands for. He underestimated this important factor. Celtic is the peoples club, and do not exist for families to feed off. It exists because they represent a culture, and when people slowly watch their culture slipping away they rise up and do something about it. And that's exactly what happened.

Conscription Time Celtic Style

If you were to name a date that will be recorded in Celtic's history for all time, it would be October 25th, 1990. The day Celtic fans became involved in club politics for the first time.

This was the day that Brian Dempsey was removed from the Celtic Board. To say it was an untimely sacking is an understatement. This was three days before the Skol Cup Final.

The fact that Celtic lost this game 2-1 to Rangers made it even worse because I think many fans realised at this precise moment that the people who sacked him were more interested in themselves than the welfare of the Club. Nobody with the Club's best interests at heart would give the Club such bad press at such a vital time.

This sacking really made me sit up and think of what was really going on at our Club. All I could smell was self-interest by the Celtic Board, and it concerned me a great deal. At this time I was standing on a street corner on occasion before and after matches, selling the fanzine 'Not The View.'

This was a popular fan's magazine and compared to 'The Celtic View' it had an opinion that couldn't be ignored. The Board quickly labelled it's readers 'malcontents', the dictionary definition of which is 'a discontented person; a rebel'. Yes, I reckon the Board probably got that just about right. But it was a big word for them and I'm not sure if they fully understood it's meaning!

In the November of that year I founded the fanzine "Once A Tim Always A Tim". Why did I start a fanzine when there already was one? Quite easy. I was watching Celtic, my major passion, slide further and further out of the picture to become an ordinary club. I also got the impression that plenty of other fans saw it this way, although there were also those who didn't, and they were, like us, entitled to their opinion.

A schoolteacher pal of mine, Derek Owen, contributed from issue number two and apart from drawing some great cartoons he also came up with some humorous writing. 'NTV' and 'OAT' were now spearheading verbal attacks on the Board at every opportunity. 'NTV' had been on the go since the late eighties and was, without doubt, the trailblazing fanzine.

If you were asked what the difference between the two fanzines was I would say we were the more militant with our direct scything approach towards the Board and all their works. That is not a criticism of NTV. It's just that more than one approach was needed to inform the supporters of our club's problems.

On Sunday, February 25th, 1991, the inaugural meeting of 'Save Our Celts' was held at Shettleston Town Hall. This was the first meeting of a rebel force, and it wasn't to be the last.

'SOC' was founded by a Clydebank man called Willie Wilson. Willie, to his eternal credit, highlighted a lot of the problems at the Club, and he did this by standing up on a platform. Not an easy thing to do, as public speaking is a bit of a nerve-wracking experience for most people at any time.

Entry to this inaugural meeting was by invitation only and around 300 fans attended. I can understand the organisers reason for the invite idea, which was to stop the meeting turning into a rabble, but when you are asking the fans to revolt you cannot hand out invitations to become a revolutionary!

It is possibly easier to say this now with the advantage of

hindsight, and it is not a criticism aimed at the SOC organisers. It is a point you can learn from. 'Celts For Change', which was born in 1993, gained experience from the 'SOC' rallies and the lesson learnt was that the door would be open for ALL to attend.

Brian Dempsey attended this meeting along with Joe Beltrami, the Glasgow lawyer, who chaired the meeting. Beltrami opened the proceedings with a letter from Christopher White which said that the rally would "Serve little purpose and simply cause embarrassment to the Club". I wonder how many words young Christopher can swallow at one time, because by the time March 4th, 1994 came along he must have eaten a good bellyful.

George Delaney, General Secretary of the Supporters Association, refused to attend after being invited, and he dismissed the rally as "a nonsense". Mr Delaney later on described the 'SOC' rally as being a bandwagon for certain people to use. You could see from these statements that certain people just couldn't, or didn't, want to see further than the end of their nose.

I often wondered through all of the campaigns why people in his position, who were entrusted to represent the supporters, just didn't want to know? Was it because they were traditionalists and didn't understand that these concerned Celtic supporters were no part-time Che Guevaras, or was it because with the sniff of possible change in the air some of their comfy arrangements would be threatened?

Lisbon Lion Jim Craig also took the platform that afternoon and looked very emotional. Jim made some fine statements and was a very articulate man in front of a mike. He said: "The Board have failed to learn the lessons of history." And that they must not "retreat behind the barricades" when faced with constructive criticism.

Constructive criticism. Another set of words the Board had difficulty in understanding. Jim worked as a commentator for Radio Scotland and it has been said that the reason he suddenly lost his job there was because of the insistence of one of the Celtic directors. I wonder who that could have been?

Brian Dempsey said something which I took notice of and have never forgotten. Brian was the master of the mike and he urged the fans to "Go that extra mile to achieve what we want and deserve as the paying customer." That type of statement is not one that slips out of your mind easily.

All of the people I have mentioned here are important because in their own small way they played a part in the eventual change which came much later. There were a couple of more 'SOC' rallies, but for some reason they lost their momentum and eventually petered out. Which was a pity because they had started something which I felt could have achieved a lot more. From memory, I think it was the last public meeting at Shettleson Town Hall that they invited the new Chief Executive Mr Terry Cassidy. Bless him, he was good for a laugh. He hit the scene as the Board's buffer-zone and it appeared to me he was completely out of touch with just about everything he got involved in.

I approached him at the end of this meeting and said to him "Excuse me Mr Cassidy, would you mind being interviewed for the "Once A Tim" fanzine?" He replied "A fanzine, why not?"

I wrote to him and we arranged a meeting for 23 January, 1992, in his office at Celtic Park. With my visitors pass pinned onto my jacket I was escorted up to his office and met by his pretty secretary Clare, whom I have since got to know quite well. We have shared glass of one wine or two on a purely platonic basis, you understand.

As I was shown into his office he was standing with his back to me as he stared out of the window. This is a tactic people will sometimes use to unsettle you and I recognised this immediately. I had no apprehensions about meeting him, as I knew more about Celtic than he would ever know, even if he worked at Celtic Park for the next 20 years.

When he eventually turned around I made sure I was still standing. This was in reply to him not actually welcoming me into his office. After all it would be rude to sit down if he didn't say so. Therefore I waited for him to say so.

Once we got underway he spoke quite openly. I asked him

if it was OK to tape the interview. This way there could be no doubt in any body's mind as to what was said. It protected him and it protected me. He agreed without hesitation and I placed the tape on his desk right in front of him.

I asked him just about every question that was relevant at the time concerning Celtic and, to be fair, he answered all of them in fairly lengthy detail. They were all printed in the fanzine, but one question I asked him at the time sounds even better today.

Q: Do you feel threatened about recent reports of a Board takeover?

A: No, not at all. Have you seen the names of the people? I would have to stick around to see them. If you want a laugh these are some of the people you want. My goodness, what's a football analyst. God almighty threatened by that lot. You must be joking.

Yes, Terry could give you a laugh on occasion. The thing is, he was serious. His office is now the typing pool for Celtic's new owners.

As I left his office we agreed that he would see a transcript before it was printed. I was pleased with this as there would then be no misunderstanding regarding its content.

As with any interview I did for the fanzine, I always had one in the can as it were. Therefore Terry's wouldn't be published until the March issue. He called me up a couple of times through Clare and asked if it was ready to read. I explained that it wasn't being published for about another month and I didn't have a room full of secretaries willing to transcribe 36 questions from a tape and edit the content onto 11 pages of full type.

As soon as this was done I would let him see the full copy, at least 2 weeks before publication. I sent Terry a letter which referred to one of our many phone conversations. He had been a touch unsavoury in some of his comments aimed at me, and I pointed this out to him. Two days later I received a reply from him. Now if I hadn't worked out previously that Tel boy was a touch paranoid, then I had now. His letter accused me of holding back on showing him the text of our interview.

Part of what he said is as follows: "My suspicion was and perhaps still is that by the time I get a transcript of the interview it will be too late to make any alterations that may be required because you will say it is now at the printers and past the deadline."

The day that I handed in the transcript we had a bit of a set-to in his office. The conversation got a bit heated when I said to him that the deal he struck with Umbro was not as grand as he had made out in 'The Celtic View', and that a club of Celtic's stature could possibly have got a better deal.

His reply to that was "Why don't you F' off out of my office?"

Well really! After being brought up in Pollok, I wasn't used to such bad language! As I made for the door I reckon he realised the error of his ways and started to talk away again.

Once I had sat down the conversation settled a little more, and I remained very frank with him. "Look Terry, there is no point in sticking up for this Board. When they have used you to serve their purpose they will sack you, have no doubt about that. They are only using you to act as a buffer zone for their problems. Don't trust them, you are on a hiding to nothing."

He retorted "Nobody will bloody sack me from in here." I said: "I will bet you £20.00 they get rid of you when they think the time is right." As I left he told me to inform Clare of our small wager and this I did as I left the building, dropping in my security pass on the way out of the building.

In between me almost getting the heave from his office, and making the bet with him I told him he should come down to my local and meet some of the guys over a beer, and he subsequently did.

He came down to Heraghtys Bar one night and sank a few pints of the Black Irish brew. He was entertaining and we all had a good laugh, but he never reappeared.

When Terry did get sacked I felt no joy. None whatsoever. But I had been proved right, and he couldn't see it. I really did feel sorry for him. They were just using the guy to deflect the mounting criticism from themselves and he was mug enough to carry it out for them and ended up carrying the can.

I phoned him about three months after his sacking to remind him of our bet. He claimed he couldn't remember, and I told him that Clare could quite easily refresh his memory for him. I don't think I have ever noticed such a change in a man's attitude over such a short period of time. He just seemed like a lost man. As far as the bet was concerned, I couldn't have cared less.

He more or less agreed with me on my opinion about his ex-employers. I asked him how he was spending his days and he said: "Mostly looking out of the window, and playing golf."

The final irony of all this was that the people who eventually paid Terry off with regards to his court action against Celtic were the very same people whom he had dismissed as a joke!

So by New Year 1993 there was no more Cassidy but a new player called David Smith had already taken the field as Vice-Chairman to cousin Kevin. His appointment was quite a departure from the norm for the Celtic Board as he hadn't belonged to any of the Families.

David Smith, who lived in Fulham, London, was the hired hand who eventually fired blanks. He had been brought onto the Board in February, 1992 to add his financial expertise to a group that didn't have any. He was to dig them out of the financial hole they had dug for themselves but was found to be left wanting. In the March, 1993 issue of the fanzine we published the results of a readers poll we had conducted:

Question 1: DO YOU WISH THE PRESENT BOARD TO REMAIN?

YES 0%, NO 83.6%, SOME SHOULD GO 16.4%.

Question 2: IF YOU SAID SOME SHOULD GO WHO ARE THEY?

100% MICHAEL KELLY, 100% CHRIS WHITE, 90% DAVID SMITH, 80% KEVIN KELLY, 40%. TOM GRANT, 20% JACK McGINN.

Other comments in this section included "Who is David Smith?" and "Pass Kevin Kelly a rope."

What these results tell you is that the fans had identified the bad guys and the not so bad guys. The supporter who had only wanted to go along on a Saturday and watch his team was now becoming politically aware, Celtic wise.

Another trophyless season had just ended. But we made it into the UEFA Cup and at the same time waved goodbye to standing in the 'Jungle'.

Fans expectations of a summer move by the Brian Dempsey-led posse didn't transpire and many supporters were left wondering why. I reckoned that the Board were hitting a real low point at that time. With hindsight the real reason was that the rebel group were still in the process of formation and proper plans hadn't been put in place.

I was coming more and more into contact with Brian Dempsey and much of the information as to what was actually going on came via my friendship with David Low and Brian. Around August, 1993 I met with Dempsey to find out what, if anything, was happening behind the scenes.

Fergus McCann had unveiled plans to redevelop Celtic Park and had distributed his 'Questions for Supporters' outside Celtic Park on match days. The plans were impressive and supporters were warming more and more to the idea of this wee man from Canada pouring money into the Celtic.

Brian told me that he was impressed with Fergus McCann's plans. "There is a pragmatism about them and it would be good to see if the various 'rebel' groups could come together."

For the first time I was beginning to wonder if, perhaps for some reason, the group were having a bit of a personality clash. But there was so much going on at the time with regard to the present Board that the last thing I paid attention to was any friction within a possible takeover group.

When I look back now, perhaps those signs were there even in August, 1993. Brian continued: "If people have Celtic's interests and are prepared to make compromises we could make a potent force, and the more money we can put together, the better."

Who was he referring to there with regard to "making compromises?" Was it Fergus or was it himself even? Or perhaps the biggest compromise of all may have been to include Gerald Weisfield in the original attack force. At this point in time the only names being seriously mentioned (remember you could be mentioned one week and never heard of again, the way things were going) were these three men plus John Keane and the former owner of General George Carpets, Eddie Keane.

But the most telling point of the conversation was when Dempsey told me that the only thing that would force an unwilling seller to sell would be if they run out of money and can no longer service outstanding debts.

Possibly never a truer word was spoken regarding the Celtic takeover because that is exactly what happened. The thing is, it didn't happen on its own. And the fight to make that happen hadn't even started at this point. All the hard work had still to be done.

With all parties mentioned, the general plan was to make an offer of around £17.5m to be put into Celtic.

Fergus McCann's package to supporters had cost him around £25,000 to produce. But I reckon it was money well spent because it let the fans know for the first time that this man was serious.

Remember too that no Celtic director had, up until this point, put anything approaching £25,000 into Celtic.

October of this year was easily to prove one of the most momentous in the club's history. The month started off with a home game against Kilmarnock with Fergus McCann attending the game. The shocking and petty antics of the Celtic directors were now displayed for the world to witness.

As was usual when Fergus hit town the press were on his tail from the word go. At the end of this match 'Radio Clyde' wanted to interview McCann but the Board in their infinite wisdom had decided to eject him from the ground. Can you imagine this happening anywhere else in the football world?

It would also be harder to imagine how those so-called

custodians could go one better and embarrass not only themselves, but the Club as a whole, any further. But they did!

Here we had a man who had flown the Atlantic and, further, a man who was willing to invest in Celtic and, who ultimately saved it, being forced to sit in the front seat of a cold transit van to explain his proposals via the radio to the masses.

The following Wednesday (October 6th) was another day in Celtic's history which eventually would prove to have a telling effect on the club's future. Celtic went to St Johnstone and lost 2-1. The following day Liam Brady resigned. He said he had made his mind up on the coach coming back from Perth, immediately after the game.

I felt Brady did the correct thing, but in saying that I felt he made his move 10 months too late. On a personal basis I had lost faith in Brady immediately after the game against Rangers on January 2nd earlier that year. Celtic lost that match 1-0 and he made the following comments after the match: "We were magnificent. That's the way football should be played. As regards us and the championship, I think the challenge is over." Yet we still had 19 league matches to play.

Well after comments like that it really was over, for him anyway. I had no time for him as the Celtic manager after those statements. His comments told you exactly what he thought was expected of him. He displayed no grief, no urgency, and had publicly shown a total lack of concern about what was going on around him.

It was thought that his assistant Joe Jordan would take over but some person in high authority at Celtic Park let it slip that the Club was interested in approaching Lou Macari, who was busy doing a decent job at Stoke City. Joe took off on the Friday morning with more dignity than the so-called custodians who were about to approach another manager and leave Jordan in the dark. It was business as usual. If there was a way to do things in a messy fashion then the present families in charge had got it down to a fine art.

The Chairman Kevin Kelly said on behalf of the Club that

"Liam had done the honourable thing by resigning". I reckon that was code for "Thank goodness we didn't have to sack him, as we would probably have had to sell a player to pay him compensation."

The support had suffered enough and, ironically, the seeds of revolution had been sown 45 minutes before the St Johnstone game even started.

Brothers in Arms

You can push some of the people some of the time but you can't push the Celtic support all of the time.

The Saturday following Brady's resignation Celtic played Dundee at Celtic Park. The atmosphere at this game was the worst I had ever experienced. The mood of the support had totally changed and you could sense a dangerous frustration in the air. The Board had for so long played on the faithfulness of the fans and I think that this game in particular was a real turning point in the supporters' attitude. You can push it for longer than you should, but it's like everything else in life. There is a fine line. The Celtic Board had now crossed it.

About 45 minutes before the St Johnstone match a Clydebank man, Brendan Sweeney, and a few mates handed out leaflets at Perth asking the supporters to have a banner protest against the Board the following Saturday. Needless to say he quickly ran out of leaflets.

I meanwhile had a new issue of the fanzine out on the Saturday. The content of a fanzine is always at the printers at least a week before it is made up into a booklet. I had decided to go for broke and write the final chapter in Liam Brady's

Celtic career and had penned, a week before he resigned, the reasons he should no longer be Celtic's manager. The front cover said "BRADY IT'S OVER." I was slightly apprehensive about taking this step because Brady was still Celtic's manager and the support might not take to kindly to this type of headline.

I gave it a great deal of consideration and decided that as I was the editor of the fanzine I would stand or fall by my decisions. In my heart I knew Brady wasn't the man for our Club. Ruled by my heart I went ahead with the cover and the summing up of Brady on the inside pages.

When he resigned the day before the fanzine was delivered I looked up into the sky and said a silent prayer of thanks!

We always had a meeting point after selling the fanzine. That day it was at the bottom of Janefield Street at Springfield Road. I stood in the street the same as the rest of the guys and shouted "'Once A Tim', always a Tim." One of my mates who sold it came up to me at half-time and said that a guy from Clydebank wanted to speak to me, "Brendan somebody." He couldn't remember his second name. "I told him you would be in Janefield Street after the game and he would get you there. He said something about leaflets or something."

Sweeney came along with a couple of mates and asked if I could put an advert in a future issue of the fanzine about the banner protest that he was hoping to organise against the Board. I readily agreed and we shook hands. Obviously at that point I didn't know Sweeney at all. But I will state quite clearly that I'm now glad I do.

Earlier that week I had spoken to Brian Dempsey and he kindly allowed me to use his offices. I had an idea, and I wanted to speak to several people that I didn't know too well, but whom I felt were on the same wavelength as myself regarding what should be done about the current situation at Celtic.

I think we all possess that instinct which tells us if we are sure about someone. For me anyway Sweeney displayed a heart that cared deeply about his Club. For a married man of 26 to finish his work and then rush up to Perth to hand out leaflets, when all he wanted to do was watch his team, told me he cared about the same thing I did. He felt action had to be taken to preserve everything we stood for.

There are talkers and doers everywhere in life. Some are easier to spot than others, but I was sure about Brendan's pedigree. He stood there with the rain running down his face and the hooped wool around his neck, as we discussed the desperate situation our Club was in. Brendan is one of these people who put everything second and Celtic first. If you asked him at any time during the long arduous campaign, to rid us of the Board, to do something Brendan would reply: "What do you want me to do? I'll do anything." Knowing what I know now, I can safely say that if Brendan had not enjoyed such a strong marriage and a very understanding wife he would have been faced with a very serious dilemma. His wife Elaine came from strong Celtic stock and this, I'm sure, helped him through a great deal of personal barriers during the most stressful points in our fight.

That was one thing I felt some people failed to realise during all of this; the personal effect it had on your life. Remember Brendan and the others had a living to earn and they were disrupting their life, on a daily basis, in order to help save our Club.

These type of people are very rare. Their goal is not money and nobody got paid for what they did. These people did what they did because they believed it was the right thing to do. When people started to put rumours around that we had been paid £30,000 by Brian Dempsey, and then Fergus McCann, it made me so angry. Here we had people on the 'Celts For Change' Committee having to put up with and cope with this when the people saying it had never lifted a finger to help Celtic unless there was something in it for them.

These rumour mongers disgusted me and still do. They couldn't even try to understand that there are human beings around who do things because they love something, and not for financial gain.

If there was a low point in our campaign then this was it. If I didn't have such strong good friends around me then this propaganda, along with the pressure that already existed, could have forced the campaign to a halt. I don't know whether people actually thought we were getting paid or were just intent on trying to create smears because we threatened some of their comfortable perks.

Thankfully we had a collective belief that what we were doing was right. I knew it was, and we had to see it through to conclusion.

A few times my confidence was at a low ebb. One particular day I was up visiting my mother. She was fully behind everything I was doing and always supported me, but being a wise woman she would also point out certain things to put me right.

She always preached "Keep your dignity at all times, and never lower yourself to the dirty tricks some of your opponents might use."

I must have been sounding pretty negative this particular day because all of a sudden she grabbed me by the shoulder and angrily shouted to me: "Are you going to let these people beat you? Are you going to let them get you down? Is that the way I brought you up? Get out there and show them, and don't ever come in here talking like that again."

At this time I phoned Brian and implored him to take legal action against the rumour mongers. He said they weren't worth the time. I wished he had, but I suppose in hindsight he had more important problems to deal with.

As I have said I even got a call from Alex Cameron at the 'Daily Record' enquiring about it. If there was a price on what was achieved then you could forget about £30,000 and start adding a few zeros.

I invited Brendan along to the meeting at Brian's office the following Tuesday. Brendan was the first of the four 'Celts For Change' committee-men to join along with myself. I can sum Sweeney up quite easily: a man born with green and white stripes on his heart.

We met at Brian's office the following Tuesday. Present were myself, Brendan Sweeney, David Low, David Watt, Paul McNeill, John Thompson and Gerry Dunbar, editor of 'Not The View'. All of these people were Celtic supporters and concerned ones at that. The idea of the meeting was to put minds together, and hopefully come up with some kind of action plan.

Various ideas were put forward and several action group names were also mentioned. My initial group name was 'Green Action' which some felt was a bit militant. I thought that this was why we were here. We were not assembling to organise a trip to the seaside!

'Celts For Change' was also mentioned but no final decision was made. This type of meeting told me that although everyone had Celtic's best interests at heart, others, I felt, did not understand the type of commitment that would be required to see this through.

From my point of view I reckoned I had a moral obligation to get involved, because I wrote about the situation in the fanzine. If you are going to do that, then you should join the fight.

We finished off this initial meeting no closer to forming a committee but I had a rough idea who would still be standing at the end of the next meeting. That took place on October 19th 1993 in the basement of McConnell's Bar, in Glasgow's Hope Street. Bill Gallacher, shareholder and uncle of Blackburn Rovers player Kevin Gallacher, was present along with a friend of Sweeney's, David Cunningham. They had both attended St Columba's School in Clydebank and had been in touch on and off since schooldays.

I had noticed Cunningham on the 'Focal Point' TV programme in 1991 where they had been asking supporters opinions regarding the situation at Celtic Park. Davie was a guy I could easily relate to and he quickly displayed the type of energy that would make him a vital member of the eventual 'Celts For Change' committee. I liked him because he looked as if he had the stomach to go the whole way, and he was coming up with loads of good points and ideas.

He ran the Duntocher Celtic Supporters bus, and I have known many solid Celtic supporters from that area over the years. They run the bus from the Duntiglennan Bar, a place I have enjoyed a right good few evenings in prior to meeting

Davie. At the end of this productive 'underground' meeting the first committee was formed.

I again put forward the name 'Green Action' but a few of the assembled thought that it was too rebellious. They pointed out that there was a terrorist group in Germany called 'Red Action' and that perhaps 'Celts For Change' was a better name.

The initial committee was Sweeney, Cunningham, Thompson, McNeill, Watt and myself.

John Thompson was the elder of the group, he had excellent communication skills and a big Celtic heart. All of the faxes and the press releases were put out through John. He also had many good ideas regarding share dealing and many contacts in the business side of Celtic. Amongst these were lots of people who had invested heavily in Celtic but were unhappy at the direction the Club was taking.

John spent an enormous number of hours attending to the paper work and his background efforts may not have been properly appreciated. He took so much time off his work to attend to 'Celts For Change' business I was surprised he was still in employment. John was another guy I could relate to easily, because he also had that vital energy and will to win attitude and in many ways was a calming influence on the rest of us when things got hectic.

This meeting ended with the above provisional committee formed and a few plans made. The first was to get a banner made (you'll know us by our sign) with our logo. The second was to get posters printed to slap up all over Glasgow 40 x 30 inches with all the Board members faces printed together with the legend, 'WANTED FOR GROSS MISMANAGEMENT'. This had a major impact and the group received massive publicity through this.

The public relations the group carried through the campaign was better than any major advertising agency could provide. This was because of the energy we had. It was incessant.

Weeks later we had another meeting in Davie's house and I was having difficulty in getting along with David Watt. His ideas and mine couldn't gel at all. At this point we had not really elected a group leader and this meeting achieved less than the two previously. I went home that night thinking that if Watt's ideas were going to be carried, I may find it difficult to carry on.

I decided the following day that I would stay on the committee but Watt would have to become the out and out group leader. I mentioned this only to the others, because if it had been said to Watt we would have had a direct confrontational situation. The group didn't need that at that point.

The others were very undecided about his plans, but I felt that if I was to lead them I couldn't implement his ideas or follow the course he felt the campaign should take. But I would still stay in the group, in the background.

This was an uneasy situation and the others Cunningham, Sweeney, and Thompson were with me. At the same time I didn't want a confrontation with Watt because he was a Celtic supporter like the rest of us, and was doing his best. Still we needed to get things sorted out and have an plan of action implemented.

I felt it was time to have public meetings. We obviously had to involve the supporters in our planned course of action, but had we agreed one? I placed an advert in the 'Daily Record' asking fans "If they cared about the future of their Club" to turn up at the City Halls in Glasgow's Candleriggs. This was around the last week in November.

Around 30 people turned up for a Hall which held 50. I and a few others spoke about the current situation. We spoke with passion and asked fellow fans for their ideas. We placed another advert in the 'Record' and booked the same hall for 2nd December, 1993. I arrived about 30 minutes before the start and couldn't believe my eyes. The fans had already filled the room and were standing in the doorway and stairway and way back out into the street. It was brilliant because they had arrived dressed as they would for a match wearing scarves and jerseys!

We were given the larger hall upstairs which held 450. By the time it was full it had over 500 inside. The press were also in attendance. I stood to speak, as did a few others. The energy in the room was electric and I was totally buzzing. The support were noisy and full of ideas and energy and we explained our rough strategy and asked them if they were with us. They were, by an overwhelming majority.

We appealed for funds to organise and pay for things like hall rental, posters, banners, newspaper adverts etc. A bucket was passed around and a few hundred pounds was collected. I can't emphasise enough the energy this gathering created. The Board had just knocked back the McCann/Dempsey offer of £17.5m to be injected into Celtic. The Board and it's supporters rejected this offer out of sight. This was the spur we needed to get stuck right into the Board. The 'malcontents' were on the march!

I went down to Heraghtys on my way home. A couple of my mates, Mark Graham and Paul Keenan, had been at the meeting. Mark commented: "Matt you don't know what you've started here. You have some responsibility on your hands."

I always remembered him saying that to me. It's not the kind of thing you forget in a hurry. Paul remarked: "You are going to get a lot of hassle. Things may be difficult for you in Glasgow now, but you will have 90% of the fans behind you."

At this meeting and at the AGM four days earlier, I had noticed the same face always asking pointed, intelligent questions with regard to the current situation. He had stood outside with his 7 year old son, and around 1,000 other hardy souls, in minus six degrees of frost from 6.00pm until the AGM finished at about 11.00pm.

This man's face stuck in my mind. How many people would bring their son along and stand in freezing conditions for five hours? They were there along with the others, hoping that the Board would have accepted the McCann/Dempsey plan to put real money into our Club. Their wait was in vain and I remember the totally dejected look on his face when he asked what had happened at the meeting. I informed him that things were the same. As usual no progress had been made.

The normal procedure for Celtic AGMs was to make your way to the Jock Stein lounge and register yourself with the waiting officials. I had a proxy for a rebel-member in Ireland and intended to use his vote.

I had entered the lounge only minutes before the start and noticed George Douglas the Celtic Security advisor waving towards me, intimating that I should walk towards him. I walked over and asked him what he wanted. Remember he worked for the Board and was perceived as an enemy of what the rebel group were attempting to achieve. Therefore I was suspicious.

He told me two gentlemen were waiting outside to speak to me. They turned out to be Sheriff Officers. I immediately went back inside and spoke to David Low. He turned to Sandy Moffat, a solicitor. I told him that two Sheriff Officers were outside attempting to serve me with a court order banning me from attending the AGM. At this point George Douglas was getting a tad impatient and was asking me if I was going outside. My answer was an emphatic "No." The two Officers entered the lounge and served me with the papers. Sandy Moffat checked them and it turned out that the signatures that were on the papers sent from the USA were not the same as the signatures sent the previous year. I hadn't a clue what was going on. The problem had happened in the USA, where the father and son of the same family and of the same name apparently signed each other's papers. Most people would notice it as a simple mistake. But the Board capitalised on this and went to the expense of pulling a Judge out of his bed to sign some papers. As it turned out Fergus McCann received the same treatment as me but he was quickly given new proxies by the rebels present. Me? Well I was allowed to attend, but not speak.

Meantime the confrontation between myself and David Watt was about to come to a head. At some point during the previous six weeks it had been made clear that I was to be group leader. I can't remember how it came about, it was that important! It happened probably because I had the biggest mouth!

Govan Town Hall was the venue for the next meeting seven

days later on 9th December. David Watt's idea was to call for a boycott of the Hibs game at Celtic Park on 18th December. I was vehemently against this. It was far too early to have any hope of success. My argument was that we should inform the support what we were all about, what our aims were and ascertain what they thought should be done. I wanted to take on board their ideas. There are always ideas and energy from the floor. It was their Club and I was not going to stand on a platform and dictate to them what was happening without consulting them.

David wanted the boycott. At this point I would have walked away if he had got his way. The entire structure of the campaign was at risk.

I spoke with the others before we took the stage. They were with me all the way as to why it was too early to call for a boycott of a game, the first time in 105 years of Celtic history, and the match targeted being only nine days away.

I think David had possibly been in touch with one or two of the others prior to the evening starting. I met him in the foyer of Govan Town Hall about 30 minutes before the start. He told me he couldn't make the all-important meeting as there was a family matter needing attention. He asked me if we were calling for the boycott from the platform. I said no. And that was basically it.

He played no further role in the 'CFC' campaign. Did he jump or was he pushed? Nobody kicked him out. He just never came back.

Paul McNeill also left that night.

I told the support, amongst many other things, that we the fans held the ultimate weapon in determining our club's future. And that if we didn't use our influence we would not have a future. I added that it was up to every fan to do something about it and that we must all work together to bring change urgently.

The meeting was very lively and I could feel the energy and the frustration even up on the stage. The following day we planned to visit the Bank Of Scotland in George Square and have a protest with placards pronouncing: 'Bank of

Scotland STOP backing a bankrupt Board' and 'Fergus McCann is our £18m friend for life'. I also phoned Michael Kelly at home live on stage in front of the 850 audience. I had seen Bono of U2 use this device on stage and I thought it would be a nice idea. When Kelly answered the phone I was delighted. The crowd went quiet. "Hello Michael, it's Matt McGlone. I am meeting with 850 Celtic fans at Govan Town Hall. We are unhappy with the way you are running our Club. Would you like to give a message to the Celtic support?"

Kelly replied: "Can they actually hear me?"

I said: "No, but I will tell them what you are saying."

His reply was: "I don't wish to take part, but have a nice evening."

Although he wouldn't speak the crowd appreciated our efforts, and we received huge applause. As the meeting carried on the speeches were all of an emotional nature, because that is exactly the way the fans felt about this great club. We asked the hall how they felt about an immediate boycott. The vote was roughly 35% for and 65% against. I judged the relative closeness of this vote as being an emotional gesture, considering the buzz that was going around the hall. I pleaded with the crowd to show patience. "We are not strong enough yet. We must march as one." The 'Celts For Change' committee had still to meet with the two other supporters groups, and anyway to boycott before you are organised would be sheer suicide. A few heckled but they only numbered around three or four.

Scottish Television and BBC Scotland covered the meeting and excerpts were shown the following evening on television. The publicity was exactly the type of positive press we needed. As one of the other lads spoke I had a minute or two to scan around the crowd. At the back of the hall I noticed Willie Haughey and Michael McDonald standing against the wall. They were now becoming players in the takeover game and would eventually become directors in the new set- up. Their presence told me that people were beginning to sit up and take notice of us.

During that third meeting I again noticed the face that had

been in the crowd at previous meetings. As he left to go I approached him and after a short chat I recognised exactly where this guy was coming from.

I explained to him that the four existing men on the 'CFC' committee were working flat out to achieve the aims that hopefully he himself held. I told him that he had been noticed at just about everything we had done so far and he was welcome to join the committee as the workload was heavy. As he appeared dedicated to our cause he was exactly the type of person we were looking for. Without hesitation he said, "Yes I will help, no problem." And as he said that the 'CFC' committee was finally completed.

I have described the other lads, but how do I describe Colin Duncan, a man who had the same attributes as the other three?

He is very solid in his belief of what he wants for his Club, and was prepared to stand up and be counted like the rest to help achieve that. Colin wanted to protect what his father had told him about Celtic. He in turn wanted to instil this identity that he had been brought up with into his own son, the son who had stood for five hours in the freezing cold with his dad. Duncan became another valuable member of the first team squad.

The following day we hit the bank. We were doing one thing right, and that was publicity stunts. They were not stunts for stunts' sake. They were carefully planned demos aimed at getting maximum coverage for our efforts. To win a campaign such as this the public had to be aware of what we were doing.

Around 300 fans stood outside the bank holding the prepared placards. Shoppers and passers-by watched in amazement as the crowd chanted "Bank of Scotland, stop backing a bankrupt Board!"

It was decided that Davie Cunningham and myself would enter the bank to get a reaction from them.

Both STV and BBC had camera crews in attendance. I approached the girl at the teller: "Hello can I speak to the manager please?"

"He's not in, can I help?"

"No, I would like to speak to the manager."

"What's it about?"

"We're having a peaceful protest outside with regard to the Bank continually propping up a debt-ridden company. If we can't speak to the manager then all of the people outside will be coming in to open accounts and then close them again."

She looked at me as if to say: "Is this guy serious or what?"

Within minutes the assistant manager appeared and he ushered Davie and myself into a rather grand office. He was very sympathetic to our views but also said he couldn't discuss the confidentiality of the customer's account.

We understood that, and that was enough for us. We had made our point. Once outside Davie and myself were hit with a battery of newsmen and TV cameras.

That evening both TV channels carried coverage of the previous evening's events and the demo outside the bank, as well as a further demo outside the Celtic Shop.

If that wasn't good enough the day's real 'pièce de résistance' was about to be announced to the nation. That evening the bank issued a statement about their role in Celtic's affairs. This was unprecedented in the Bank's history and was put out at peak viewing time.

'CFC' were now becoming a powerful force, eliciting maximum publicity. Our new recruit from the evening before turned up at the bank wearing dark glasses even though it was a damp and cloudy day. The reason for this was because Colin had taken a day off work to attend the bank demo, such was his commitment to the cause, and he didn't want his boss to notice him on television. Perhaps it's just as well we didn't take him into the bank!

Our next tactic followed hard on the heels of the three the previous day. Celtic were playing St Johnstone the next day, 4th December, 1993. The idea this time was to take the giant 'BACK THE TEAM, SACK THE BOARD' banner into the Rangers end of the ground. As this was not a big-time fixture, we asked the supporters not to attend that part of the ground. This would enable us to have the end empty and the banner hanging there on it's own. Again creating publicity, with the Board being unable to miss our message.

Brendan, who works for Scotrail, was unable to attend the bank demo due to shiftwork but had been entrusted to take the 60ft banner down to the launderette to get it ready for it's big day. I don't know what type of washing powder he used but I got a phone call saying: "Matt the sign on the banner has washed off!"

Davie Cunningham had spoken to Brendan and told him the grim news. Davie said Brendan was close to tears. We had a 60ft piece of material with no message on it.

So here we have the big day planned. The press had been informed and would be turning up with cameras. The fans would be getting leafleted outside the ground and we have a 60ft piece of cloth and that's it! Let me tell you Sweeney's phone must have been down with a virus because no matter how much Davie and I tried to get through it just wouldn't connect!

The situation required calm and sane thought. The facts of the matter were that there was no signwriter available and it was a job that would take an entire day. I met with Davie and his pregnant wife, Siobhan, in McConnell's bar. I had been on the phone to Margaret McGinlay, wife of Celtic player Pat, about an unrelated matter. When I told her of our calamity she showed immediate concern, shouting across the living-room to Pat: "Pat don't we have some white paint down in the garage. Matt's banner has washed off in the laundry. Have we, have we?"

The more Davie and myself discussed the situation, the more I had to get through to Brendan. Davie told me he was distraught, but at the same time we had a situation to sort out and he couldn't be contacted. The best idea we came up with was to attempt to follow the outline of the print which was barely visible. But this would take hours.

The following morning Davie, John Thompson and his daughter went down to B&Q and bought loads of white paint, masking tape, and huge brushes. They took the banner to Duntocher School hall and worked frantically, following the faint white line.

They eventually finished at 2.00pm, one hour before kick off time. Davie had also caught up with Brendan. As it turned out Brendan spent the next three days swearing on the lives of just about every member of his family in an attempt to convince us that his phone really was out of order, and not off the hook!

The lads arrived with the banner. So too did twice as many Celtic stewards who had been instructed not to let the banner into the stadium as it would only embarrass the directors.

It became clear that there was no way we would be allowed in. We then ushered the skinniest fan up a nearby close and almost stripped him of his clothes. The 60ft banner was then wrapped around him. Barely being able to breathe properly, he was wrapped in a light raincoat borrowed from another fan, and our Michelin man was ushered towards the turnstiles. He beat the security cordon, his face almost blue, but he couldn't manage to fit through the gate. It took a steward to rescue him as the crowd clapped and cheered.

Around 200 people attended that part of the ground, compared to the usual 2000. Another success! 9 out of 10 observed our call. Our next stunt was a belter! Sweatshirts were printed for the next home game against Hibernian each with a giant letter printed on the front. One had a 'B' the next an 'A' the next a 'C' the next a 'K' and so on. The message when all 28 people were standing next to each other read 'BACK THE TEAM, SACK THE BOARD'. When they turned around the message read 'BEAT THAT MICHAEL'. The fans wearing them turned every now and again. Absolutely brilliant! Let's face it, the stewards could hardly turn a fan away just because he has wearing a sweatshirt with a letter printed on it!

Fergus McCann had came, had tried, and the Board, deep in debt, did not want his money. He told the media that he was going back to Canada as there was nothing more he could do. Although he said this and I'm sure he meant it, I privately thought he would be back. Simply because there was no way the Board could continue to run a Club that had no money, and was not making any, as each day went by.

Brian Dempsey arranged a leaving party for Fergus at the Hospitality Inn in Glasgow. Brian hired a suite on the eighth floor and to my surprise he invited myself and a partner along. I must admit I was a touch overawed to be in such company. Ten couples in total were invited. Business types who were all involved at some stage in the campaign.

Brian stood and spoke warmly of everybody in the room. Meantime, I was watching each person getting up to speak as it got nearer and nearer my turn to stand up in front of the assembled.

Nervous? I was shaking too much to be nervous.

Anyway I stood up and spoke about the non-business side of the Club, and what it means to be a fan. That was it. Nothing fancy, just emotion. Brian arranged a couple of gifts for Fergus. One was a tartan golf hat for Fergus to wear instead of his trademark bunnet!

At the end of the evening I was explaining to Fergus that my partner was not my wife and that I was not married. Jokingly he said he couldn't find a wife in Canada. I replied that if he returned to Scotland with £10m then I would find him a wife! Fergus has a great sense of humour that is not shown to the public at large. When he asked me for a business card I told him I didn't have one. He replied that he knew a place in Phoenix, Arizona which could print 1000 cards for 12 dollars. I asked him to get 1000 done and said that I would square him up later!

In the meantime the Irish support had been in touch and were keen to get the 'Celts For Change' committee over for a rally along the same lines as those we had held in the City Halls and Govan Town Hall. The problem was that there would always be a security concern about holding our type of meetings in Belfast or anywhere in the Six Counties. There was always Belfast City Hall, but I reckoned it would have been much safer up the Falls Road. There was however nowhere big enough in the Falls Road to cope with our rally.

I suggested that we go over to Belfast then conduct the rally on the ferry when the Irish supporters were travelling over to Glasgow for the New Year match (the one with the flying Mars bars!). We could have it as we all travelled back across the Irish Sea to Stranraer. Now I would consider this to be a real test for us, considering the time of year it was and the time of day it was being held. 8.00am on New Year's morning was the time, and the Irish Sea was the place! Jim Mervyn of St Michael's CSC in Belfast organised the whole show and had a band to entertain the supporters who were in good spirits.

This was another energy-charged atmosphere and plenty of suggestions on what to do with the Board came flying at us thick and fast. Some were a bit unconventional shall we say, but effective all the same. Celtic supporters all over the world are unique. They give undying commitment and solid faithful support to a cause even though they had been let down so often for so long under the old regime.

When you look at the travelling the Irish fans in particular have to endure, just to reach Glasgow, it brings it all back home to you how solid Celtic are across the Irish Sea. Celtic must always look after this type of commitment because so many people in that part of the world are dependent on everything we stand for.

Even at that time in the morning, and considering the festivities that went on the night before, the Irish bhoys were sending a charge of energy and emotion throughout the boat as it headed over the sea towards Scotland. In many ways these people were warriors embarking on a mission that they had carried out many times previously. The commitment of the Irish support has to be seen to be believed.

With me on the makeshift stage were Davie and Colin. This meeting differed from the type we had been used to in Glasgow and on dry land at that. The crowd were standing less than two feet from where we were conducting the meeting. They were also at the side and behind us. A few times one or two thought that they could perhaps take charge of the mike, but with a party hat on their head and a bottle of Budweiser in their hand! I managed to convince them I would be staying in charge.

On opening the meeting I explained that they, the fans, were the ultimate weapon, adding that anyone on the boat who seriously thought Celtic would be a success under the present Board were seriously mistaken.

I pleaded with them to stand shoulder to shoulder and fight for our club's existence, the alternative being that shortly they may not have a club. I continued, adding that this wasn't scaremongering and that the Club were £6m in debt and losing money as we spoke.

One fan asked how far back would it set the 'CFC' campaign if Celtic won the League and the Cup. My answer to that was quite simple. It wouldn't set it back a centimetre because we all wanted to win the League and Cup .The thing was, even with possible success around the corner, the fans now knew the difference.

I gave them an example. The week after Celtic beat Rangers at Ibrox Lou Macari was in charge of his first game for Celtic at home against Partick Thistle. The crowd, according to the Board, was 21,000. That tells me that the supporters were sufficiently scunnered, and that they had lost faith in them.

One fan asked the supporters to put their hands up if they backed the 'CFC' campaign. I found this a curious question. Perhaps I just assumed that they did. Any doubts I may have had were quickly dispelled as it was 100% support. We attempted to phone Chris White from the ferry but got no answer. Two immediate shouts were: "Give us his number and we'll phone him later!" Another one: "He's probably out rowing!" (Chris's favourite sport). Overall the meeting lasted an hour and a half. The boat then rocked a bit more as the support finished off with a couple of rounds of "Hail, Hail!". Me, I was about to start enjoying my own New Year, but not for long.

Unfortunately this Old Firm game was about the worst I have ever experienced. Celtic went a goal down in minutes and ended up going in at half time 3-0 down.

The pent-up frustration amongst the supporters was evident, and Mars Bars and hot pies flew into the Directors Box from uptight fans. Now, nobody can condone violence but there are reasons for everything. It must be remembered that this Board, through their mismanagement of the Club, had, in my opinion, totally exasperated decent supporters almost beyond a level where any reason could be shown. The fans were totally and utterly frustrated and I really felt, as I sat in the Front Stand, that there could be real trouble brewing.

It is only human nature for the man who loves his club so much to react when he is forced to witness his team go 3-0 down against his biggest enemy. You would be inhuman not to show anger.

Thankfully the fans and their minds kept together until the end and the support headed home, wounded but not dead.

Five days later we met with the Affiliation of Registered Celtic Supporters Clubs at the Watermill Hotel, Paisley. Colin picked me up from the house and we were to join the others at the hotel for the meeting at 12 noon. As we drove towards the car park we noticed STV and BBC camera crews waiting at the entrance. Hazel Irvine was there for the BBC and I said to Colin, "I bet she gives me a kiss when we say hello to each other." "No chance!" was his reply.

"I'll bet you a fiver," I said. Now if anything was sure here, then it was my fiver, and without fail the bashful Hazel delivered. Colin shook his head, accompanied by a wry smile.

This was the first time the two groups had met and to be honest I expected nothing. That's exactly what we got. To achieve success in a campaign like that you had to be radical and push that bit harder than the rest. Sitting back and accepting the soft option will never bring change, and neither will sitting around thinking about it, hoping things will change by themselves.

Our attitude was forceful and constructive. The Affiliation were certainly good Celtic supporters but I always had that nagging feeling in my mind that although they thought we were right in what we were doing they couldn't adopt such a radical approach to the problem. The leader of their five-man delegation, Peter Rafferty, did most of the speaking and did listen to what our proposals were. In these type of situations you need more Hawks than Doves. Our committee were made up of five hawks. If I was to describe Peter I would say he was a dove and although he wanted change at Celtic a more radical approach was needed to solve the problem.

At every 'Celts For Change' meeting the entire committee spoke, unlike our counterparts, where their leader did most of the negotiating. At the end of this gathering Peter agreed to put our proposals to the member clubs of the Affiliation. Our proposals were: a possible boycott of future home matches and to take part in the demonstrations we had organised at home matches. Now to take part in a demonstration was obviously a personal choice. What was being asked here was for the Affiliation committee to recommend their members taking part. He was aware in any case that some of his members were already attending our demonstrations and rallies. This meeting constituted another day lost at work for us all.

In between all of this I had written to Celtic's manager Lou Macari, principally to explain to him where we came from and what we were trying to achieve. I also wanted a face to face meeting with him to enable me to work out what side of the fence he was on. It was important to know this, considering the amount of information that was filtering through our group. Friend or foe, I wanted to know! He phoned me on that day and asked me to come over to Celtic Park at about 6.00pm. There was no time to assemble the entire committee but I did manage to get hold of Davie and up to the Park we went. Lou's attitude was pretty laid back. He had obviously been fed some Board propaganda as he was sure that it would all be sorted out without any kind of takeover. I assured him that it wouldn't. He told us both that if anyone was really serious about offering that kind of money then why didn't they go on TV with it all piled up in notes and say "Here is the money, we want to take over the Club."

I explained to him that I imagined company takeovers were not achieved in this manner. I now realised this former boyhood hero of mine really didn't have any kind of grasp at all of what was going on. I think he perceived us all to be people who were unhappy and who would make a noise and go away after a week or two and not come back.

How wrong he was! We were dug in so deep we weren't going anywhere until we had achieved victory. That was the bottom line. If any of the five of us had given up in the middle of this struggle we would have walked around torturing our minds for the rest of our lives, contemplating what could have been achieved.

We left Macari's office with the promise from him that he would speak to the Board and try to arrange a face to face meeting with them. Now just in case Lou had this down as a throwaway comment perhaps to appease us, I made sure he wouldn't forget and it was on the back pages of the Press the following morning just to remind him of his promise. More good publicity for the group.

Billy McNeill wrote in 'The Sun' the very same day: "If the fans felt something positive was happening they would give their support. But the Board have got to be open and honest. They are not dealing with idiots here.

I've spoken to quite a few people in the 'Celts For Change' group and they are not hooligans or mischief-makers. They are decent, honest-to-goodness Celtic fans who believe the Club needs to be restructured. They care about the Club," he continued, "My message to the Celtic Board would be: Stop ignoring them. Go out and listen to what the various supporters' groups are saying. The strength of feeling may come as a shock.

Anyone at Celtic Park who thinks that these people are an unrepresentative minority is wildly off the mark.

It's high time steps were taken to sort out the whole mess.

Communication between the Board and the fans would at least be a start."

Now that came from the former captain of the Lisbon Lions, a Celtic manager on two occasions and a lifelong Celtic Legend! Those comments were a great boost to the lads at a time when some heads needed lifting.

The following day we held a rally at the City Halls in Glasgow with around 1800 in attendance. On the platform, apart from ourselves, was Peter Broughan a Celtic fan and shareholder who later produced Rob Roy, the film starring Oscar winner Liam Neeson. Peter had come along that Sunday afternoon simply to attend the meeting and I asked him up to speak after spotting him sitting in the crowd. He spoke with passion and was warmly received by the crowd. This was a particularly emotional and passionate meeting and the atmosphere was full of positive energy.

I was proud of the way all of the lads stood in front of this enormous crowd and belted the message out from the heart. They were all just working-class Celtic supporters who had no time to get used to learning the rules of public speaking. They stood and they spoke from their hearts and they conquered. On some occasions, minutes after a meeting had ended one or two of the five would end up rushing to work to start a shift.

This was Colin's first major speech in front of such a huge crowd. Although he had spoken on the ferry this was his first in a hall and as you stand looking at so many faces it can be a very intimidating sight for somebody not used to such an occasion.

Like the rest of the lads on their maiden speeches he turned out to be a natural. Solid as a rock.

The Battle Goes On

The meetings were now really taking off but one of the big problems was finance. We needed money. If it hadn't been for the generosity of the support when we passed the bucket around at meetings we couldn't have held a meeting. Here's a rough example. The hire of a hall could cost between £250.00 and £500.00. A small advert in a newspaper to advertise the meeting could easily cost £120.00. There were also printing costs amongst other outgoings.

I had been in touch with Charlie Nicholas and asked him if he would attend our rallies as it would be a great boost to the support. He told me that he couldn't as he would get into trouble at Celtic Park if he was seen at them. I didn't want him up on the stage. I only wanted him to sit in the audience, but the answer was still no. Our conversation ended at about this point, when he said the doorbell had gone and he would have to go. If Nicholas or any other player wanted to stick their heads up and support us instead of making the occasional wee comment in the press then this was the ideal opportunity. They didn't at any time and this really saddened myself and the other four tireless workers who were at breaking point on more than a few occasions. It wasn't such a long time ago that

John Robertson, the Hearts striker, but a boyhood fan of Hibs, risked the wrath of his employers and his supporters to attend a 'Hands Off Hibs' rally at the time when it seemed that Wallace Mercer may succeed in merging both clubs.

On March 4th 1994, the takeover day, Charlie walked out of Celtic Park shouting his mouth off to the press when it was all done and dusted. That was dead easy for him. It's just a pity he hadn't done it when the fight was taking place. We were all pretty disgusted at his behaviour. Charlie Nicholas wasn't part of the 'Celts For Change' campaign, and don't ever be kidded that he was. He had the opportunity and didn't want to know. It's all right dancing around in the press when it suits you, saying a wee bit here, and a wee bit there, but we knew who stuck their heads above the parapet and he was not one of them. I had known Charlie for a good number of years and this disappointed me. In 1982, when he scored 52 goals for Celtic, my twin sons were born. One is called Nicholas.

On Sunday January, 16th, 1994 we had our well-publicised meeting with the Affiliation and the Association at the Association headquarters in London Road.

For some obscure reason, because Davie was a member of the Association their President Jim Brodie said that he couldn't attend the meeting. I argued that Davie was an important member of our committee and that I wasn't dictating who was in their line-up. The choice here was that this all-important meeting was going to be abandoned if we persisted in having Davie present. I honestly don't think I had ever heard of anything so ludicrous in my life.

I told Mr Brodie that we were going outside the room to discuss whether any of us would attend the meeting if Davie was not allowed to. We eventually agreed amongst ourselves that if we allowed their pettiness to dictate and cancelled the meeting it would only scupper any hopes we had of all supporters groups working together.

Meanwhile Davie went outside to speak to waiting journalists, amongst them camera crews from ITN in London, there for a national news report. This meeting was held because some members of the Supporters' Association wanted their committee to meet with us in the faint hope that we could all work together. I, like the others on our committee, hoped we could but we didn't enjoy the best of relationships with their committee.

In fact at this first meeting I said that this struggle for Celtic was not about holding onto "comfy seats", referring to the cosy arrangement that allowed the Executive of the Association to sit in the Directors Box at every home match. This brought a shout from their Vice-President, with whom I hadn't yet been in conversation with. He shouted at me: "He's a wido, get him out of here!" I asked Mr Brodie to control his language as we were trying to conduct a meeting.

The meeting was strained. We all spoke. Colin, myself and Brendan. John Thompson was also a member of the Association and decided there was no point in attending, as they would then have told two of us to leave the meeting.

The following Wednesday we were to meet with Lou Macari and hopefully the directors. From our original meeting with the manager the three supporters groups had been invited to a further meeting. Not surprisingly the Association failed to show. We had been informed that the Celtic Board had been in touch with the Association that afternoon. Their excuse was that they had a finance meeting that evening. That evening Celtic were playing Aberdeen.

As I made my way to Celtic Park for the 4.00pm meeting, I bumped into none other than Michael Kelly as I turned the corner of Gordon Street and Buchanan Street. I said to him "I will be seeing you at Parkhead in 30 minutes." He replied "Och Matt, what are you telling the press now." Needless to say he had no intention of appearing at the meeting, and neither did the Association. At least the Affiliation turned up, represented by Peter Rafferty and Mick Dinning. For 'CFC' there was myself and Davie. For the Board there was Tom Grant and Lou Macari. No matter your opinion of Tom Grant, he did have the decency to turn up and listen to both groups. It was asked at one point how many of the Board we wanted to remove. I replied: "All of them."

"You can't have that," came the reply.

"Well, we shall just have to wait and see," I said.

I told Tom that the campaign would continue and we would stop at nothing. The meeting more or less achieved nothing but at least it had taken place. I went outside and spoke to Chick Young for the BBC and the story went out on the 6.30pm news.

Lou Macari apparently received a verbal outburst from Chris White for daring to act as a peacemaker. As we left Celtic Park the Association Vice-President entered the building along with Celtic director David Smith. Both were people who couldn't or wouldn't attend an important meeting set up by the manager but somehow found the time to enter the ground together at around 5.10pm. This strengthened my resolve and only confirmed what we all knew. The Association committee were in close contact with the Celtic Board.

The first meeting between us, the Association and the Affiliation ended with all agreeing to meet the following week. It was also agreed that this joint statement would be read out: "The three groups agree to work together to resolve the problems that exist at Celtic Football Club, and we all agree that change is required at the Club. A further meeting to formulate a plan of action is scheduled to take place next week."

This was only agreed after we insisted on more forceful wording on the original mealy-mouthed statement, and even the above is hardly radical. I had no doubt after attending this meeting that next week was going to see a parting of the ways. None of the official bodies had the same attitude to the problem.

At this period there was no point in delaying the inevitable. We invited the other two groups to the Kelvin Suite at the Grosvenor Hotel in the West End. Hugh Pym, who was the Scottish correspondent for ITN, was there, as were the BBC and SKY. Hugh, who is now on News at Ten every night, is an ex-English public schoolboy, and a really nice guy. He was familiar with all the 'CFC' lads as we had spoken many times on TV with him.

He came over and said: "Matt, your group have wonderful

public relations, which company do you use?" I looked at him as if he was perhaps winding me up, but he wasn't. I replied: "We don't use any company, we do it ourselves."

He couldn't understand how we could get so much good press during the running of the campaign.

Our team on this day was myself, Davie, Brendan and Colin. We all sat together in the room waiting for each group to arrive.

Colin was joking around and said: "Well if it gets hot in here today at least I've got a bottle of water to cool me down," as he held it above his head. Unfortunately for him the cap was loose and it went spilling down all over him, minutes before the start of this important meeting. We had been quite tense prior to this but we all just fell about laughing! The perfect tension-breaker!

As the Association committee entered the room Jim Brodie wasn't pleased at the seating arrangements as we sat around the table.

"Is this some kind of tactic?" he enquired morosely. Everybody else was quite happy, but we altered the seating arrangements just to enable the talks to go ahead. I was about to open the meeting (being the Chairman for the day) but again Brodie interrupted, saying he wasn't happy with two alleged press reports reputedly contributed to by 'CFC' regarding the previous week's meeting.

We didn't have a clue what he was talking about and told him so. Eventually we got underway as we attempted to help sort out our club's problems.

The Association's proposal was to ask fans to write a letter to the Board explaining the reasons why they should step down.

The Affiliation suggested that they ballot their members on the idea that they pick a home game, pay the entry fee and leave 60 minutes after the game had started, no matter the result at the time.

'Celts For Change' said that we had resisted calls for a boycott from supporters since our meeting at Govan Town

Hall on December 9th, 1993. Since then we had met with the team manager, a Club director, some of the players and the Association and Affiliation supporters' committees. We had also consulted individual supporters who didn't belong to any organisation. We felt, therefore, that we had exhausted every avenue in an attempt to achieve change without calling for supporters to withdraw their financial support.

We intended to release a statement calling for action at the forthcoming home game against Kilmarnock on the 26th February. I also added that we didn't want to get sucked into weekly talks which were going nowhere, especially with the close connection the Association committee had with the Board. The stalling was over and our cards were on the table for all to see.

As far as we were concerned these two committees were happy to stall and go around in circles for weeks. I asked them to join us with our action as many members of both their groups wanted a boycott and stated that they were present at these meetings to represent their members.

Jim Brodie said we had wasted his Sunday afternoon and he was leaving the meeting. Peter Rafferty said they were going also, but at least had the courtesy to thank us for the hospitality we had arranged. Mr Brodie accused us of entering the meeting with a prearranged plan. Well thank God we had some kind of positive plan of action instead of some unworkable plan to send notes of protest to a Board who would bin them before they even read them! To say we were disappointed by both committees would be an understatement.

We had taken time to consult them on important Club matters and they just wanted one worthless meeting after another. We were the group holding public rallies and getting the support, with halls packed out wherever we went. We were the group who didn't have comfortable seats to protect. Instead we were out every night of the week attempting to find solutions for our Club. We all put personal relationships at risk and neglected our children. We were the guys who took time off our work for the sake of Celtic, and those who paid in every week to support our Club. We had to put up with every type of lie and smear and Brodie tells us we have spoiled his Sunday afternoon!

They only got involved when Celtic supporters in their organisations got totally fed up with their lack of action and told the committees to meet with us.

They had their constitution. We had the support. I know what I would rather have. The supporters helped bring change at Celtic, not outdated constitutions.

The following evening Jim Brodie said in the 'Evening Times': "It would appear as if no solution is acceptable to them if it does not include Brian Dempsey and Fergus McCann. If they are working for that consortium they should say so."

This statement prompted one of the 'CFC' boys to take legal advice as he had never met Brian Dempsey or Fergus McCann. The same applied to some other 'CFC' committee men.

If both these committees felt they had something comfortable to protect, something that perhaps they thought earned them esteem, they should have considered the future of Celtic Football Club's wellbeing before their own personal gain.

When both those two groups walked out of that room and left us sitting there we knew it was up to us, and anything else that would happen thereafter would be carried out only by us. The talking was over. We were now ready to take that final step and make the final push.

It is hard to describe the scene after they left. The few of us who remained sat stony faced. The meeting had been difficult as Jim Brodie was a very experienced campaigner when it came down to negotiating positions.

At this moment in time tempers were a bit fraught amongst one or two of us because of certain things that were said or rather I felt should have been said, and the bawling and shouting was coming from me.

Looking back now, with the benefit of hindsight, the 'CFC' lads had been through a lot and perhaps I was expecting too much too often. They had all done more than their best over the previous months and we were all now feeling the strain from inside our own homes and the offices and factories which we also had to frequent.

In any case we had work ahead of us and a tough decision to make.

As the three TV networks continually banged on the suite door I felt we all had to sit down and regain our composure before we went out to finally announce our ultimate weapon, which was to withdraw our 'financial support' from the Club and to ask the support to back us all the way.

After many months of organising rallies, demos and meetings, now was the moment to go for broke. We had so much to lose, but even more to gain for our Club. We all spoke of the one reason we all got involved in the first place, and why we must now go ahead with the final push, despite the two official organisations refusing to back us. What must be remembered here is 10 committee men from two organisations were seen to be representing thousands. From this group of ten only Jim Brodie and Peter Rafferty spoke when we negotiated. I asked for opinions from the other eight, only to be told they wouldn't be commenting as their two leaders would handle all the talking.

This I found very strange. What is the point in attending a crucial meeting if you are not allowed to talk? All of our guys spoke. It was decided that Davie would read out the statement to the press as we had always attempted to share the spotlight at times like this. It read: "This is the saddest and hardest thing we have ever had to do as Celtic fans. During the past months, 'Celts For Change' have listened very carefully to the demands of the Celtic support.

"The Celtic support want change and they want it now! They are tired of empty promises! They want money spent to provide a winning team! They want to stay at a refurbished Celtic Park.

"The current Celtic Board cannot deliver any of these things! The Board must resign. Only by their removal can we hope to bring about long-term success at the Club again. All areas of compromise have been exhausted. We feel that every

Celtic fan must examine his or her conscience to take action at the home game against Kilmarnock on the 28th February 1994 by withdrawing financial support."

I don't think I have ever felt or looked more ill in my life when that statement was read out. The strangest feeling engulfed us all, because it seemed such a negative thing to ask of the support, i.e.: not to go and watch their team. But for the long term good it had to be done. It was read out to ITN, STV, BBC, SKY, various radio stations and to the newspaper men in attendance. The four of us sat at the table in a state of shock. The following day Hazel Irvine (BBC) came to my workplace and interviewed me at lunch time.

She asked many questions, one of them being what would happen to 'Celts For Change' if the fans didn't heed the boycott? In fact we never actually used the word 'boycott'.

I answered that the group had carried out a lot of painstaking work and the fans now had a wonderful opportunity to show the Board they meant business, but what would happen to the group would be difficult to predict.

I wouldn't admit it to her, there and then, but I reckoned we may well have slipped away if the Board had maintained support from the fans after all of our campaigning. The difficult part for the fans was distinguishing between the Board and the team. They were paying money to watch their team but were being asked not to in order to hurt the Board. I felt if we could get through that barrier then we could well be successful.

At this point my long-term girlfriend Elaine and I planned a week's holiday in an attempt to resurrect what remained of our crumbling relationship. It is difficult when you are in the middle of a campaign such as ours to recognise the true effect it is having on your partner. Constant phone calls, in the 'Evening Times' case from 6.45am onwards for the benefit of the lunch time edition; cancelling of arrangements; being constantly approached by people asking what's going on; and never being around when I was meant to be; plus all the rallies and campaigns.

We booked a 7 day holiday to Los Cristianos in Tenerife.

Seven days of no football; no phone calls; no meetings. Just the two of us.

So there we are holding hands at the Glasgow Airport check-in and a guy on our flight taps me on the shoulder and away we go. "Hey Matt, what's happening with the Board?"

What are you supposed to do? One thing I have never done is ignore anybody when they are asking a Celtic question, never.

The second day, we are lying on the beach chatting away. There is guy and his wife lying nearby, he says: "It's not is it?"

I dipped the 'Ray Bans' and said: "Aye it is!"

I was frightened to turn in Elaine's direction, half expecting one of her special looks! The guy turned out to be Des McKeown, who played for Celtic reserves in the late 1980s and who at that particular time was with Albion Rovers.

If I was to be totally honest with you the damage was done well before the holiday. Some things in life are irretrievable and no matter how we both tried the campaign had laid waste to our relationship.

Life in Glasgow was becoming more and more difficult. Walking through the city's divided streets can be very unkind to an ordinary punter whom nobody recognised four months earlier. There were many incidents. One day I was walking through Buchanan Street at lunch time. As a gentleman in a suit passed me he stopped and asked: "Was I not Matt McGlone?" I nodded and he let fly with a torrent of abuse which went along the lines of: "Ya dirty Fenian B!" this was repeated several times amongst some other choice epithets.

What am I supposed to do? Turning a blind eye and biting your lip turned out to be the best remedy. My friend Pat McGinlay, at the time a Celtic player, got similar treatment as he stood in McDonalds with his daughter. The way I look at it now is that it goes with the territory.

On February 2nd we headed for a rally in the Coatbridge Town Hall. The Coatbridge lads are a solid bunch who backed 'Celts For Change' the whole way. They were magnificent in their backing and at the end of all the hassle the campaign brought all the 'CFC' committee were invited to the Kirkshaw Kangaroos CSC Player Of The Year dance. The Coatbridge Bhoys were amongst the first supporters to motion the official Association that their committee should meet with us. I don't forget commitment like that.

From there we moved, four days later, to Dundalk, in Ireland. Two of the main organisers were Jim Mervyn from the St Michael's CSC club in Belfast and Mark Burke from the Naomh Padraig club in Dublin.

There were 52 delegates representing over 5,000 fans from all over Ireland. Myself, Davie, Brendan and Colin drove over via Stranraer and Larne. Perhaps it was being in the border town in Eire, perhaps it was just one of those days, but everybody was in top form. Here we had four men informing the Irish of, hopefully, our final act of the campaign.

All the lads spoke with emotion and we painstakingly put over all our points in an emotive fashion. I think Sweeney, in particular, had his finest hour. We just couldn't get him to shut up. At the end of our talk we did a question and answer session and then the Irish decided to vote on whether to back our campaign or not. From the 52 delegates present 51 voted in favour of a total boycott. One bus had still to consult its members but a day later they had also backed 'Celts For Change'. I was jubilant. A couple of the lads went off to speak to the radio stations present and also, via the phone, to a station in Belfast. Mark Burke stood and proclaimed: "The entire nation is behind you."

The meeting had been a great success and at last a small chink of light could be seen at the end of the tunnel.

After the meeting ended a fair few of the 200 strong crowd came over for a chat. Many of the fathers had brought their sons along and asked for a photo to be taken with their boy. This to me was an honour. Somebody wanting their son photographed alongside me?

This particular man from Belfast had spoken away for quite a while and as they left I gave his son the Celtic badge from my lapel. I remembered myself at that age. Anything with Celtic on it was treasured. The day had been long and the meeting, like most, was mentally stressful. We decided to visit the bar and with the work out of the way we had a great evening. We were staying at the Imperial Hotel and there was a wee guy collecting glasses who looked about 12 but claimed to be 18. Every time he visited the table to remove the debris we gave him the opportunity to win £1.

"Right wee man, heads or tales?" And if he won we gave him the £1. Halfway through the evening all he had to do was shout one or the other and he was on to a pound. At the end he was collecting glasses from our table that he had brought over himself! He must have made about £30 from us. Generous to a fault us Glasgow boys!

At the end of this brilliant day we all decided to act like real adults and spray the outside of each others room door with shaving foam! I'm afraid I couldn't reveal what was written, but suffice to say it would have been a good idea to have it rubbed off by the morning, certainly before the chambermaid arrived!

To our horror when we all got sensible again in the morning, the shaving foam had somehow managed to discolour the paint on the door. When you rubbed off the foam, the message was still there! I, of course, had nothing to do with this and was rudely awakened to be informed of their deeds from the previous evening. Honest!

The chambermaid was none too pleased but we crossed her palm with some notes of the Republic and she changed her frown into a smile. Let's face it, if it can do that to paint imagine what it could do to your face if left on overnight? Not that you would go to bed with your face covered in shaving foam!

TV appearances, demonstrations outside the ground, rallies and leafleting continued right up until the planned day of "withdrawing our finance".

Colin and myself went to visit Willie Haughey and Michael McDonald to explain our strategy to them. Willie told me that he doubted whether the support would observe the boycott and that it would possibly spin back in our faces. This meeting took place about a week before the planned action.

Gerald Wiesfeld and City publican Paul Waterson were all part of a group which included Willie and Michael. Their plan was to buy out the directors with the money mentioned being £3.6m. Both Colin and myself pleaded with them to hold off on the offer because we were sure the boycott would be observed and they wouldn't have to pay people off for practically running our Club into the ground.

The strain of the campaign was getting to me a bit at this point. I was in conversation with Brian Dempsey and happened to mention to him what was going on around about me.

He said to me that there was no point in being the most self righteous man in Glasgow if it meant not having a friend in the world. "Always look after your health and your family," he said. Good advice and I appreciated it, but it was easier said than done.

We had a meeting arranged for the City Halls two days before the proposed boycott. On the evening of this meeting I drove out to Paul McStay's house in Uddingston to find out the players' reaction to the boycott. Paul's opinion of the Board wasn't much different from ours. I told him we needed the support of the players and that they had to get more involved. To my surprise Paul asked when our next meeting was. It was arranged for Monday March 7th. He said there was a good possibility that the entire team, without any prior announcement, would walk onto the stage as the 'Celts For Change' boys were talking and stand behind them wearing the Club blazers.

This was absolutely brilliant news. I was trying to take it all in and at the same time understand the significance of what he was saying. Can you imagine the scene? A hall full of cheering Celtic fans, us up on the platform, and the team standing behind us. Paul and myself agreed to keep it quiet from the press and anyone at Celtic Park. As I had the total confidence of the lads on the committee I told them just prior to going on stage that night. Just the jag you need two days before the make or break match.

I had asked Brian Dempsey to stand on our platform a

few times previously but for one reason or another he hadn't. This time, though, he agreed and as usual Brian struck up a brilliant rapport with the support. This was our last call to the support and although we had full backing from the 1800 in the hall we reckoned that for the boycott to succeed there had to be less than 10,000 at the game.

Brian took me aside after the meeting and informed me that he was of the opinion that the Board were likely to accept the £3.6m offer from the Wiesfeld/Haughey group. This was money going straight into the pockets of the directors. Something none of us wanted. Why should they be rewarded for almost running the Club into oblivion?

We were always of the opinion that when they went it should be with as little as possible, and certainly nothing approaching £3.6m. Because after that payoff the new owners would have to pay almost another £6m of debts that the old Board had incurred.

Then they would have to find money to bulldoze the old stadium and raise capital to build a new one. And then there was the question of raising more cash for the manager to rebuild the team. The question of whether or not to keep Lou Macari would also have to be addressed, again an issue involving money.

The £17.5m offer from the Fergus McCann group was a better deal for the Club but a worse deal for the directors.

When the takeover was finalised a week later the directors who took the money and ran, namely Smith, Michael Kelly, and White were paid a lot less than they would have received from the Haughey and Wiesfeld group.

The following morning I received a phone call from the 'Daily Record' who asked if I was going to the press conference at Celtic Park at 10.30am. I knew nothing about it but guessed that the £3.6m offer to the directors was going to be accepted.

I phoned Willie Haughey at home and said: "I believe congratulations are in order." Haughey replied: "Matt, I don't know what you are talking about. I know nothing of any press conference. In fact, I'm just out of the bath sitting in a bath robe."

If it wasn't about that, then what could it be? It eventually turned out to be another deflection from the real problems that existed at Celtic. A new company was to be formed, with a 25,000 share issue raising £6m. They also claimed to have underwriting to the tune of £20m from a bank called Gefinor for the Cambuslang dream stadium which was to be built on toxic land.

For the guy in the street it was a lot to take in all at once. I received a call from BBC's Sportscene programme which was to go out live on Friday evening at 7.00pm. I agreed to take part but I was thinking that I had better find out what this bloody Board were on about. Following a few calls I felt I had the general gist of what was going on.

But would the fans buy this idea? This was the day before the boycott. This was what the Board hoped would finally kill us off less than 24 hours before our planned action. I knew that the programme was watched by millions and I had to get my facts right.

Prior to doing all of this I had to do my job running a small dry cleaning and delivery business. On this particular day I picked up a bloke's dinner suit which he told me he needed back for that night, without fail. "No problem," I told him.

"I'll need it for 8.00pm at the latest, I'm going to a dinner dance," were his last words. The guy was wearing a Rangers top and I felt he was sort of looking at me as if he knew me.

The only other customer I had to deliver to that day was Peter Grant, who lives near Coatbridge. My planned itinerary was: Grant's house, followed by the BBC studio and then onto the customer in the Rangers top. As you can imagine I had a lot on my mind this particular day. Elaine had also flown the nest and the pressure was really on. I delivered Peter's clothes, had a quick chat and off I went. It was now about 6.15pm and I had to get to the studios for no later than 6.45pm.

I was driving along the road about three miles from Peter's house and there are about 200 things going on in my head at once. All of a sudden I glanced into the back of the van and couldn't see the Rangers fan's suit. Then I realised that I'd delivered it to Peter Grant, who had told me he was just going out. I frantically dialled him and the telephone rang and rang. Just as I was about to hang up he answered.

"Hello Peter, it's Matt. Listen I've delivered a man's dinner suit along with your order."

"Matt, I'm just walking out the door."

Now you can imagine the scenario. The Rangers top doesn't have a dinner suit to wear to his night because Matt McGlone picked it up and left it in Peter Grant's house! Can you see me explaining that to the Rangers top? And by the way I have to be sitting talking live on the telly, looking composed, 8 miles away in 30 minutes, and I have still to dive into the back of my van and change superman style from my jeans and tee-shirt into a suit, shirt and tie.

Peter agreed to dig out the suit and leave the porch door open for me to pick it up. I made it to the studio. A quick make-up and it was on with Chick Young and Alison Walker interviewing.

As the programme unfolded, myself and a business analyst, Bill McColl, were to come on live after Willie Haughey, Brian Dempsey and Michael Kelly had spoken. Willie was very angry but composed. He said that a meeting to buy shares in the Club had taken place with Vice-Chairman David Smith.

Smith issued a statement that day, saying amongst other things that he was "...not aware of any director who had sought a buyer for their current share holding. I know that over the last two years numerous unsolicited approaches have been made to individual directors to sell their shares and all have been rejected."

Haughey said "I sat in an office at Dickson Minto last Friday evening at 11.00pm. Present at this meeting were David Smith and Christopher White and various company partners. At this meeting in front of two lawyers, David Smith guaranteed that no matter what Kevin Kelly or Tom Grant wanted to do, he could deliver his group's 40% of the share holding in the pact. For this we deposited £3.6m in a bank account, of which David Smith's lawyers, Dickson Minto, had clarification.

"I also believe this was put forward to the Board at a meeting sometime last week and this is where the problem with Kevin and Tom arose. For this man to make this statement is a disgrace to Celtic Football Club, and they should know what they are dealing with."

Dempsey was next up and said, slightly cryptically: "Here we have a situation today where they are talking about Celtic Football Club going public, shares being purchased by we do not know whom, under written by we do not know what, for which purpose we are not sure. Here we have once again Cambuslang trotted out, always miraculously at a crucial time before a boycott, and when the bank is exerting pressure."

Brian confused almost half of the nation with the first part of that statement!

Michael Kelly was next up and part of his statement read: "His view was that the directors should not profit by selling their shares, and that has been my consistent view. Any money that is available should be put directly into the Club, and that is what I appeal to Willie Haughey to do. The members of the pact do not want to accept his £3.6m, they want it to go into the team," adding, "I think the supporters and the media will applaud that because that is what they have been asking us to do: don't take the money, put it into the Club."

At this point I almost fell off my seat laughing at Michael Kelly, but at least he had seven days to change his mind.

Next up was one of the Board's reserve players, Lou Macari, who said: "I will take money for players from anyone, even from David Murray." Which was a perfect cue for me to come in live: "Lou said there he would be interested in taking money from David Murray. I wouldn't be and I don't think any Celtic fan would be. Michael said there that Celtic had listened to the rightful demands of the fans. The rightful demands of the fans aren't to hive off Celtic to the highest bidder, a financial institution, but that's what's happening here. The Celtic fans are losing total control from this idea. If this £6m comes in from new shares it is coming from financial institutions, it's not coming from the guy in the street. It's not coming from the fan. It's not coming from the person who wants to own this Club."

Alison asked: "How does this affect your boycott tomorrow? Does it still go ahead?"

I answered: "Yes, most certainly the boycott still goes ahead. Willie said there that the fans have got to understand what they are dealing with here. We have said this all along. The fans have felt deceived today and the boycott will go ahead, even more forcefully now. I must emphasise here that this is not a good deal for the fans. It's a deal that brings money in and takes control away from the fans. Celtic will just be like John Browns or ICI, being a Plc company. The team would just be part of a Plc company."

At the end of the programme it was into the back of the van, suit off and jeans back on and up to the Rangers top's house in the West End. He answered the door and the programme following Sportscene was on in the background (this was 15 minutes after I had been on). He say's to me as I make my way down his path: "Hey mate, don't I know your face?"

If he knew where his suit had been hanging an hour earlier, then I would have probably been hanging beside it!

That evening it was snowing heavily and I was back to looking out of the window, praying that the game wouldn't be postponed after all the preparation we had done for the boycott. It was, and I couldn't believe it. I thought of Michael Kelly dancing around his living-room. This was a crushing blow.

Eight miles down the road at St Mirren's ground they played the game after clearing the snow off the pitch. Celtic, with undersoil heating and all the resources a big club has, didn't even make the effort. That lunchtime I was on Scotsport extra time with Peter Rafferty from the Affiliation, and Haughey was on with Michael Kelly who was still attempting to sell his wonderful share issue to the support. The dialogue was much the same as the previous evening on the opposite channel.

The boycott game was rearranged for the following Tuesday, March 1st, 1994. Don't forget the date! The League rules state that postponed games must be played on the first available midweek, and Kelly and Co. were running out of blizzards to save them! It was also announced on the Monday in the 'Evening Times' that the Gefinor Bank that Celtic said was providing cornerstone funding for their Cambuslang dream was, in fact, not doing so at all. In the UK they operated from a small London office via a faulty answering machine. Events had now turned full swing. The press were full of the bungled attempt to float the Club and our boycott was due for tomorrow. Now it was my turn to dance around the living-room!

As usual we were one step ahead of the Board. I suggested to the lads that we hire a reputable market research company to count exactly how many fans were entering the ground. Our feeling had always been that it would be less embarrassing for them if the crowd figure was above 10,000. We kept it totally secret, just in case the Board attempted to move the counters on.

If we hadn't appealed to the support for finance at meetings this tactic would never have been possible as it didn't come cheap.

The night before the boycott I didn't sleep. Everything went through my mind. Everyone we had met; every meeting; every demonstration; the commitment from the lads; the effect it had on my family; the parting of the ways between Elaine and myself; the effect it had on me. Was I the same person mentally that started this campaign? My friends were right down-to-earth people and I'm sure that if I had changed they would have been the first to let me know. My mother, touching 70, had been right behind me the whole way. If we lost tomorrow how would she feel? As I collected all my thoughts I realised that yes, no matter what happened the following day, even with the personal cost, it was still all worth it. I had met some great people who felt the same about the Celtic as I did, and that was important to me.

The following day I was on the ITN lunch time news, linking up live with Peter Sissons in London. I appealed to the supporters who were not going to the game to stay away from the stadium as the last thing we wanted was confrontation between our own fans. Hugh Pym, the ITN Scottish correspondent, promised to send £50.00 to the 'CFC' fund for the interview as we had one or two bills to pay regarding the campaign.

That evening myself and the lads were invited out to the Royal Bar in Coatbridge along with Willie Haughey and Michael McDonald as the game was going on. The hall was full of people who would normally have been at the game. It was an encouraging sight.

In the car on the way to Coatbridge we were excitedly listening to 'Radio Clyde's' Davie Provan who said that with 10 minutes before the kickoff there were 4000 to 5000 in the ground. We all let out a huge roar, shook hands and hugged each other.

We were all aware that some Celtic fans were notoriously late in going to games and that this figure would rise. But not by much.

Celtic didn't know we had the crowd counted and released a crowd figure of 10,888. The following day I went to the Scotsearch office to be given the official attendance figure.

They had over 25 people covering the gates and their figure was 8,225 which included 1,905 in the away part of the ground. That meant 6,320 Celtic fans attended the game. That season Celtic had just under 7,000 season ticket holders. So how many people actually paid in for a game that could have attracted around 23,000?

I reckon that game cost the Board approximately £150,000-£200,000. If they hadn't taken notice of the support prior to this game then they had to now.

That evening we were again on the BBC news with the document from the research company and we also had the back page of the 'Evening Times'. My comments were: "The boycott was a major success. The Board will lose even more money at their next home game unless they listen to their customers. The point has now been made to both the directors and the Bank of Scotland. Now is the time for action."

Brian Dempsey said: "Last night clearly demonstrates the feelings of the supporters. The Board should realise the fans have no faith in them and they must resign now before any more damage is inflicted on the Club."

The Scent of Victory

The following evening I was sitting at home watching TV, 'Minder' was on. Then came a news flash on national TV. It read "THE CELTIC BOARD HAVE QUIT".

I honestly thought I was seeing things. I threw my hands in the air and just jumped about going wild! I had a friend down from Dundee staying with me, Sarah-Ann Boyle. She must have thought I had taken a fit. She might have been right!

For the next three hours between 10.00pm and 1.00am my phone never stopped ringing! I wanted to party and I phoned Heraghtys Bar and asked Pat Nellis the manager if he could put a huge carry-out in a taxi and send it up to my flat. I also asked him if they had any champagne. As if Heraghtys would have any champagne! Minutes later Dempsey appeared on TV. About an hour later I phoned him at home and he assured me it was "all about to happen".

I then spoke to Dominic Keane for over 30 minutes and he confirmed it. "Tomorrow, Matt, is the day." Another of the calls was from David Low. We had fallen out in January during a period of high tension in the struggle for Celtic and I had no further contact with him, until the last day. "Hi Matt it's David.

We've beaten them!" I replied: "I know, I can hardly believe it." I decided to bury the hatchet and forget about our serious difference of opinion.

One of the phone calls I received was from Eileen Marino from GMTV in London. Her call went something like this. "Hi Matt, it's Eileen Marino from GMTV News. I would like to interview you with regard to tonight's news about Celtic." This was at about 1.30am. I asked her when she wanted to do it. She replied, "Well, I'm in Edinburgh at the moment. I will be at your door with a film crew at about 3.30am." I said, "Listen, don't come to my door at half three in the morning. I'm about to go to my bed." She pleaded: "But I need this for the 6.00am news." We eventually agreed that as long as she didn't chap my door with a film crew at 3.30am I would go to Celtic Park in time to do a live link-up to London in the car park. Just to make sure I didn't sleep in she agreed to send a taxi for me at 5.30am. I am normally not a good riser, but I could smell victory and was high on adrenaline.

At 5.30am a taxi didn't arrive, but a limo did, complete with a driver in leather gloves and hat opening the doors for me. Over the top, certainly, but I was intent on soaking up every minute of it. Up we went to Celtic Park and I spoke live via a satellite link-up to London with Penny Smith for about 6 minutes. I then drove around the East End of Glasgow with the chauffeur until it was time to do the 7am news live. Did you know you can't get a cup of coffee in Glasgow before 7am? These programmes were going out nationwide. The country was wakening up to a piece of Celtic history and I was still trying to take it all in.

At 9.20am I went to Dempsey's office to be met by Low, Dominic Keane and Brian. Brian warned that "it may not be all over today" and to prepare for "five days of hell."

Low strutted about the office with his St Aloysius' tie on. I needed the victory that day, and Dominic looked almost assured.

The actual money paid to the Bank of Scotland that day to save Celtic the indignity of receivership was £1m. This amount was paid by Fergus McCann alone. The money had to be wired from the USA and transferred from dollars into sterling and paid over at the Bank's branch in Glasgow's St Vincent Street. The paperwork was finally completed at 11.52am, eight minutes before the Bank's 12 noon deadline. Five days later, on March 9th, Fergus McCann deposited another £4m with the Bank of Scotland. This was to pay the debts the previous Board had built up. What happened to all of the other men who proclaimed to have money in the country at the time? Why was it left to Fergus McCann to go through all the hassle of changing money into different currencies? I was outside Celtic Park from about 11.00am. There were about 500 to 1000 people there at any one time. Dempsey came more or less on the hour to inform the waiting fans that it wouldn't be long before an announcement would be made regarding the takeover. TV crews and radio vans were on the go all day and an announcement seemed no nearer.

At 2.13pm a red BMW drew up. Inside were Fergus McCann and David Low. Both had been at the bank and were arriving to do a deal with the Board who were now on the run. As the car arrived the press rushed forward and the car ran over the foot of a journalist.

The car was totally surrounded by TV and radio crews and scores of newsmen.

As Fergus stepped from the car, being jostled about, he looked over in my direction and said: "Hi Matt, I've got your business cards with me!" This was said as every press and TV man in the country was pushing and shoving around the car asking questions about the takeover. It was "Mr McCann this" and "Mr McCann that." As all of this was going on I was kinda glad he never pulled the cards out there and then!

McCann headed for the front door to be met by Dempsey and both men went inside the building. As I watched Fergus disappear through the front door my mind went back to the day they put him out of the building five months earlier. But here they were now sitting around a table wanting his money, well three of them were anyway.

Colin arrived at about 3.00pm and Davie about 4.30pm, both straight from work. Brendan was at work as was John. At about 6.00pm Dempsey again came to the front door and said: "There is nothing to be concerned about but it will all take a little longer." Obviously with all that was going on we would have preferred to be on the inside of the building instead of the outside. And we managed to do this, all three of us about 10.45pm. I got inside first with the help of a Glasgow journalist. Colin got in pretending he was a sound engineer with SKY TV and Davie was an assistant with a radio crew.

So there we were, all three of us inside the building, and what a magic feeling it was. We were inside the castle we had been trying to take for so long. The room we had managed to get into was where the eventual press conference was to be held, which is now the sponsors lounge at Celtic Park. Brian came out from time to time, and on one occasion he spotted me, saying: "Hello Mr McGlone, your looking very pleased with yourself tonight." I was just sitting amongst the waiting press. Like them, waiting for the announcement that our Club was at last out of the clutches of the families who had ran it into so much debt and almost out of existence.

A steward made his way over to me and said: "Mr Douglas (Head of Security) wants to know what you are doing here, as you don't have any press credentials." I pulled the steward gently towards me and said: "You go over and tell Mr Douglas that I'm a personal friend of Mr Dempsey." At that point there was nobody going to put me out of that room without a major fuss developing and I reckoned they knew that. After all we had been through we more than any one else deserved to be there to hear the words that would finally confirm, officially, that change had taken place.

In fact we went one better than that. The three of us walked over to the window and stood with our hands joined together, held aloft, proclaiming victory to the frenzied crowd below. All during the campaign we had been told to move off the pavement outside Celtic Park as we demonstrated against the Board, so this moment was so sweet. I then phoned my mother from the room to let her know what was happening. She was as thrilled as we were as I relayed the up-to-date situation to her.

At 11.15pm on March 4th, 1994 Dempsey entered the room and said that Michael Kelly, Christopher White, and David Smith had all resigned as directors. In other words they took as much as they could get for themselves on the way out from a company they all had a hand in running down.

Dempsey and McCann then made their way down to the front door where by this time the rain was lashing down on the hardy Celtic souls below. On their way down Fergus passed David Smith. Their eyes didn't meet. McCann headed for the door and said "Goodbye Mr Smith."

"Good night, Fergus," came the reply.

Dempsey stood at the front door with his arms raised, like Jesus on the hillside outside of Jerusalem with Fergus by his side. And he then proclaimed the words that I'm sure had gone through his head many a time.

"THE GAME IS OVER. THE REBELS HAVE WON."

That was a wonderful moment for us all. I wept along with Davie, as we both hugged each other and got lost in a sea of soaked bodies. Everyone around danced and kissed total strangers, the same way they had done when I was a boy standing at games with my father during Celtic's great European Cup nights. All these thoughts went through my mind as at least three minutes of mayhem continued. My Father had been dead for 14 years but maybe he knew all about our campaign and was urging me on, realising that he was one of the main reasons I got involved.

In hindsight, shouldn't it have been Fergus taking the plaudits on those steps as he was the guy who settled the account at the Bank of Scotland. I reckon I know the very reason Brian had to do it, and I'll go on to explain.

The following Monday, March 7th, the victory rally was held at the City Halls in Glasgow. This booking had been made two weeks prior, and was intended as a meeting to discuss the effects of the boycott. But the boycott had done its job and so had Fergus McCann.

We placed an advert in the 'Sunday Mail' the previous day and mentioned who would be attending. I had spoken to Brian and it looked likely that Fergus would take the stage.

I also phoned Willie Haughey because, although his group had missed out on taking over the Club he had made an effort in removing the Board and would very possibly have a part to play in the future, which has turned out to be the case. I also made it quite clear that Gerald Wiesfeld, Michael McDonald and Paul Waterson were all very welcome on the platform.

We got in touch with Hugh Keevins to compere the evening's events and warned people in advance to turn up early. To give you an idea of how busy it was, the hall held around 1700. People were lined up all around the walls, and we had to arrange seats on the stage behind us, and that was at 6.50pm, for the start at 7.30pm.

At 7.30pm the police informed us that there were several hundred outside and that they had closed the doors. They advised that they would have to move the support on from outside, as the street was being blocked.

Hugh spoke about the campaign and what the fans had achieved and the role they played over the previous difficult months.

I cast my mind back to my earlier involvement as a young Celt, including a scenario eternally etched on my mind. And, once again I was walking up London Road with my father, tightly holding his hand, watching those floodlights get bigger and bigger and both of us about to witness those great Celts, and because I am in the crowd, I am also part of the action.

That night, Monday, March 7th, 1994, as I walked onto the stage at the City Halls, I saw Jimmy Johnstone, Bobby Murdoch and Bertie Auld. They were all part of this night, our night, the 'Celts For Change' victory rally. Walking down those steps towards them as they clapped is something I will always cherish.

First introduced onto the stage were Willie Haughey and Gerald Wiesfeld to tumultuous applause. Next up was David Low who took the stage to great applause with his clenched fist raised aloft.

Following Low came three of everybody's heroes, Murdoch, Auld and Johnstone to an absolutely crashing wall of clapping and cheering.

Hugh then told the crowd that the very reason they were all there that night was because of an organisation called 'Celts

For Change'. I reckon the lads felt at their very best at that point but their proudest moment was when they all walked onto the stage to be introduced one at a time.

For an ordinary fan this is indeed a wonderful moment, because you are taking the cheers from your own folk, the Celtic supporters, and in amongst them are three Lisbon Lions. This wasn't a night for long speeches as the guests were many, but as all of you who were there know Colin decided to give it the Gettysburg address and he still gets reminded about it today!

Willie Haughey rose to speak and was a couple of minutes into his speech when all of a sudden Brian Dempsey walked into the hall. The result was bedlam and unfortunately for Willie he was halted in full flight. Dempsey walked through the hall like Jesus on water (copyright Brendan Sweeney). A certain Lisbon Lion swears he saw David Low press a button on his mobile phone which was lying on the table. The thought was that Low had pre-dialled Dempsey's number and he was sitting outside waiting in his car. If this was the plan, and I'm not certain it was, this would have alerted Dempsey to the fact that Haughey had stood to speak. Now if that wasn't the case then it was indeed some coincidence.

Now if somebody said they saw this happen they could have been mistaken. The phone could have been lying on the table and Low happened to be touch it. I'm not sure about this one, but I will point out three things. The first is that I doubt if Brian would normally walk into a hall when a speaker was addressing the crowd. Secondly, it would also be unusual for him to walk in the front door as he was a very popular guy at the time and would usually have been mobbed. And thirdly: why did David have a mobile phone with him at such a meeting? I have asked David this several times and he has constantly denied it. So the jury's out on this one.

The meeting was emotional. It was also a celebration, and several fans mentioned afterwards that it was just like being at a cup final. This was the end for us now and Brendan said that knowing he had played his part in the 1994 Celtic revolution is something that will always keep him warm at night. I think that spoke for us all.

McCann and Dempsey

At the end of season 93/94 the 'CFC' committee were invited to be guests of the Club in appreciation of their efforts.

Most were season ticket holders and had therefore paid up front anyway. I had a word with the lads and we decided to make a donation of several hundred pounds towards the Club out of our own pockets, simply to keep the status quo; that everything we received, we paid for. I would imagine that was pretty unique at Celtic or any other club. To hand out guest invitations and then be paid back for the invite. In the guest lounge we would come across some of our adversaries who would look over at us, as if to say "Look at them now, accepting guest tickets," unaware that we actually paid our way. Unlike those who still accept the free comfortable seats, sausage rolls and wee cups of tea, even after change has come about. The very change they obstructed throughout our campaign.

Even now their hands are still out: "Gimmie, gimmie, gimmie."

They say in life small things matter more than bigger things. This was brought home to me as we were about to walk off the stage at the City Halls for the last time at the end of the victory rally. It was an evening that poured out so much emotion, and it was hard to take in all at once considering the table of people we had been sitting with.

Fans had been up on the stage and we had all chatted for ages and the happy feelings had replaced the tiring months of depressing campaigning. A guy in his early 30s came over to me, offered me his hand and pulled me towards him and we both hugged. He said "Matt I was at the first meeting and every one since. Thanks." He took his scarf and wrapped it around my neck and walked away. I was totally choked. For me that meant as much as anything during our struggle and it's the scarf I wear to games today!

Brian Dempsey stood on the platform at the victory rally and thanked Willie Haughey, Gerald Wiesfeld, Michael McDonald and Paul Waterson for their contributions. I'm sitting there thinking, "He's got to thank the lads. He's thanked all the money men, but these working class guys at the table achieved more without money. He's got to thank them." But he never did, and as I looked at their faces I couldn't help but see their disappointment as they bravely tried not to show it. I wasn't bothered on a personal level, although it would have been nice, but the others would never have the opportunity again.

I am not one to keep things in as they would just burn away at me. I had to speak to Dempsey about this, and I did. He said he was sorry and that he had forgotten. Forgotten? I'm sorry, but I can't accept that. He was standing on our platform, at our invitation. It was our show and he forgot to say thanks to the hosts and achievers.

In an attempt to rectify his 'forgetful gaffe' he invited all five of us to his office. He thanked all of us very nicely, and pointed out that we had all achieved something in our lives. The fact that we did it all without looking for recompense made it all the better. That was nice, but it would have been better coming in public. It would have made them up, if you know what I mean. He gave us all a bottle of champagne and off we went.

The day after the takeover I spoke to Brian and he said he had been at Celtic Park that morning prior to the game at Perth. He was at the ground for press pictures mainly for the Sunday papers. One of the Sundays wanted himself and Fergus to pose face to face with the Parkhead frontage in the background. Brian said to me that "as soon as we fall out, (he and Fergus) they will draw a big crack down the picture."

That was the last thing I thought was going to happen. I couldn't contemplate it after everything that everyone had been through. I was convinced it was a united front. But it didn't turn out that way.

The questions must be asked. Why did it all turn out so very different and why wasn't it McCann and Dempsey together?

I was pretty close to the situation and the way I will describe it is the way I saw it. In my opinion Brian's expectations were different from what he was offered after the takeover. Now we are talking serious money here. Fergus was the man who saved the Club alone on March 4th after changing currencies from Dollars to Sterling and handing over £1m to the Bank of Scotland. He was also the man who, alone, handed another £4m to the Bank of Scotland five days later.

In between these two transactions taking place Fergus sent Brian a letter inviting him to join the Board and become a director. I know this because I saw the letter. At this point I also saw a very angry Brian Dempsey standing in front of me. This I couldn't figure out and I asked him what the problem was. Surely this is what he had always wanted, was it not? To become a director of the new Board? I asked him there and then. Was it because he expected to be offered the Chairmanship? His answer was "No." Well I'm still none the wiser.

His contribution to the campaign was a fairly major one, but let's not forget that many others made big contributions also. The fact is that he has not contributed financially to the new setup from Friday, March 4th onwards. On the other hand, Fergus McCann, in two days time, would contribute a total of £5m.

Now I think at this stage of the game you have to put your money on the table if you want to be part of the show. It turned out he didn't and that is why he is not involved today.

My view is that Brian expected to be made Chairman. I may be wrong but that is my opinion. That is not a position I would imagine is given away for free! I also think a big part of his fight was also to get even with Michael Kelly, although he would never admit this.

Kelly had been extremely instrumental in Brian's removal from the old Board in 1990 and I reckoned a fire burned in his belly because of this.

I found all this disharmony extremely disappointing. After all the depression and elation we had experienced we then had all this and it made me pig-sick. My mind went back to our last night together at the victory rally. Brian said: "All people must come together to recreate the Celtic Football Club we all know and love. There can be no battle of egos, there can be no battle of power, there can be no conflict of personalities, there can be but one goal. That is the wellbeing and future success of Celtic."

Quite. The answer to all of this is in that statement. I'm sure you have worked it all out by now.

Celts After Change

The battle was won in March 1994. What do the 'Celts For Change' think 20 months later? I asked them all in October 1995.

DAVID CUNNINGHAM

Sitting in the impressive North Stand on October 14th, 1995 during the game against Hibs, Matt asked me, "If the same crisis situation arose with Celtic again, would I be prepared to get involved to the same degree to turn it around again?"

In an instant I replied "Yes". During the late part of 1993 until spring 1994 I was involved in 'Celts For Change'. I met Brendan (whom I had been at school with but with whom I had lost touch) outside McDiarmid Park on a miserable October night.

He was giving out leaflets trying to arrange a banner protest against the old Board for the next home game. He had been in touch with Matt and invited me to a meeting in McConnell's Bar the following week. The rest you will have already read in the earlier parts of the book. At the time my wife Siobhan, a lovely girl from Belfast who I love dearly, was pregnant with our first child.

Although she had a 'good' pregnancy, as most people understand it is a difficult time for a woman, feeling unwell and suffering mood swings. She needed my help and support. At the height of the campaign I was at meetings six or seven nights a week, which put a tremendous strain on our marriage, and ultimately caused many rifts, some of which have still to heal. The bottom line is that I nearly lost my wife and the beautiful boy she give birth to in May 1994.

Therefore why did I answer "yes" to Matt's question? There are two reasons. Firstly, I have supported this Club since I was three years old and I am now 28. I remember all the good times: winning leagues and cups and travelling to all the big European nights, home and away. During the early 1990s it was no longer enjoyable watching Celtic. In fact it was like doing a penance.

The Club I loved so much was dying on it's feet and this was breaking my heart. I hope we never have to go through that scenario again. Our Club with all it's history and tradition, is too big for that to happen.

Hopefully with proper businessmen with real money running our Club we will never have to endure such indignity again. People still ask me today why I put so much effort into the campaign when I had so much to lose. The answer is easy because Celtic have always been a major part of my life, and it would have destroyed me if we had gone down the tubes and into extinction. I really couldn't imagine a Saturday afternoon without Celtic. They mean too much to me.

I now look around at the great new stadium and witness big money signings on the park and watch the potential grow in front of me, and it makes me feel very proud that I played my part in helping to bring around change at the Club. And I don't think it will be long before we are back amongst the best in Europe.

Reading that you have to ask yourself how many people would inadvertently put their own family through so many personal anxieties, as Davie just mentioned. It was his commitment above and beyond the call that helped make the campaign the success it was.

COLIN DUNCAN

Towards the end of 1993 I felt the supporters' tolerance and patience had been tested to the limit by a Board who failed to recognise that a total change of direction was the only way forward. I personally felt that they didn't care about what the faithful support thought or said. Well those days of being gullible and following blindly were fading fast.

Kelly, Smith and White to me were really despicable people. When the Board refused to accept without any reasonable explanation the offer of £17.5m from the Fergus McCann consortium the only people who could achieve change were the supporters. After I stood outside Celtic Park in temperatures of minus six with my seven-year-old son Stephen for nearly 6 hours I decided to go along to the next 'Celts For Change' meeting on December 2nd at the City Halls in Glasgow to hear what their plans were and how they hoped real change could be achieved.

I was pleasantly surprised how quickly they had organised themselves and how focused they were on what the real issues were. The following week, December 9th I attended their meeting at Govan Town Hall and I was even further impressed by their positive plans of action. At the end of the meeting Matt came down off the stage to speak to me and said that he had noticed me at all of the previous 'CFC' meetings and at the AGM. He asked me if I wanted to get involved and I said "yes" immediately. I was only too willing to help remove our Club from the clutches of the self-preservation society who were pretending to run it. My view was that the Club had to be returned to its rightful owners, the supporters.

Within a short space of time my entire family life was about to change. My wife Helen and son Stephen were immense in their support for what I was doing. It seemed that every spare minute of the day was taken up with meetings, travelling, making constant phone calls and lots of other things.

Financially it also took it's toll. It seemed all my spare cash was taken up on phone calls, petrol, and carry-out food as we seemed to spend our entire lives out of our own homes. It annoyed me greatly when I read Alex Cameron's report in the 'Daily Record' that the group were supposedly given £30,000 to run the campaign. The people who put these stories about are sad and it makes my stomach turn when I think of what I sacrificed.

My wife helped me out a lot with various small costs I incurred with all the running about. They all add up. In a way I was being selfish to my family by ringing up these extra costs, giving my family an extra bill for the sake of helping Celtic. The fact that they rarely complained preyed on my mind as many nights passed without me seeing my son. I hope he will understand. He now has his own season ticket and sits beside me in the new stand. I would like to take this opportunity to thank my boss Stevie for allowing me to change my hours around on a constant basis, and make so many phone calls.

On the question of whether I would do it again. I have met so many great Celtic fans and listened to their stories regarding Celtic and the sacrifices they all made, and I have felt humbled on many an occasion. But unfortunately the answer has to be no. The sad fact being that so many people in privileged and influential positions seemed to worry more about comfortable seats and the like, than they did about Celtic's wellbeing.

But enough of the negatives. Here's to the future of Celtic, and to the people who stood up to be counted when it mattered.

Again a story of a family being affected by the love of a club. Colin Duncan is one solid guy who would help others before he would help himself. The campaign was lucky to find a guy like him.

BRENDAN SWEENEY

In October 1993 , I would have described myself as your ordinary, happily-married, happy-go-lucky, happy-enough punter-at-work sort of guy. One thing was eating away at my soul though, and that was that the Club I was destined to support from birth, through my Irish parents, was being dragged to its knees by the incompetence and gross mismanagement of a board of directors intent on putting their own interests before that of our Club.

It was patently obvious that my feelings were shared by the vast majority of Celtic fans, as the chants of 'Sack the Board' grew louder and louder. The support though would have to be organised and under one banner for maximum effect. So I decided to take the bull by the horns. The day that was to change the rest of my life was October 6th, 1993. I got 600 leaflets printed calling for a banner demonstration against the Board, and distributed them at Perth against St Johnstone.

I met up with four diehard Celtic fans: Matt McGlone, David Cunningham, John Thompson and Colin Duncan. 'Celts For Change' was born, and for the next six months I was on the biggest emotional roller coaster of my life, culminating in the euphoria of the takeover on Friday, March 4th, 1994. For me to explain the feelings I experienced during the ups and downs of the campaign in such a short space is almost impossible. However I will attempt to convey the elation, the disappointments, the happiness, the sadness, but above all, the pride in being a Celtic fan during the biggest turmoil in the club's history.

From day one of this campaign I was under no illusions about the amount of time and work I would have to put in for the fight to be a success and I was fully prepared for it. However the worst part for me was the strain it was putting on my wife as she sat alone in the house, night after night. Meanwhile I was trying to combine my shifts with the railway, with fitting in meetings. I can count myself lucky that I am blessed with a wife who is also steeped in our tradition and understands that Celtic are my life. During the struggle the thing that drove me crazy the most was the small minority who would say we were giving Celtic a bad name. More than anything that really hurt me.

Our fight was never against Celtic, it was against the Celtic Board who were destroying Celtic. Hence the motto: 'Back the team, Sack the Board'. I often got down but bounced back just as quick, as I always knew what I was doing was right. One of my tasks was to look after the mail, and it came in from all over the world to our PO Box. Apart from letters of encouragement from Scotland, we also received mail from Ireland, the USA, Canada, Australia and England. Just reading the letters would take up most of my night, never mind attempting to reply to them.

Although I never felt like chucking it, letters of encouragement would rekindle the fire in my belly, and keep recharging the faith in my heart. My greatest disappointment without a doubt was the attitude of some people who were in a position of power to unite the supporters.

It still sickens me that some of the people who opposed us are still receiving freebies at our Club.

The dirty tricks and rumour-mongering by certain people were also a disgrace. How they can still show their face in public, never mind around Celtic Park is beyond me? If I have any regrets it is that there wasn't a restructuring of supporters clubs immediately after the takeover and a confederation of clubs formed as a priority.

Another disappointment for me was Brian Dempsey, whom I had great faith in, and who I had pictured in my mind as the original saviour. If he had any differences of opinion with Fergus McCann, then they shouldn't have caused any split. Brian always said over and over that it wasn't about personalities. If he had any money for shares in the Club then it should have been put in for the good of Celtic. As always, the only loser was Celtic.

On a lighter note I did have many laughs along the way with a great bunch of guys, especially after our meeting in Dundalk in the Irish Republic. And of course Colin, pouring the water over his head and right down his shirt! We were all in stitches, minutes before one of the most important meetings in the club's history.

On the opposite end of the scale, calling the boycott was of great sadness to me. We had put it off time and time again. It was breaking our hearts but it was our last option. In the end we consoled ourselves with the fact that it had to be done for the good of the Club.

I also had many proud moments . How else can one feel, addressing up to 2000 Celtic supporters and speaking from the heart? The joyous scenes at the victory rally were particularly satisfying. Also, sharing a platform with people like wee Jinky, Auld, Murdoch, Haughey, Dempsey and Wiesfeld is something I will never forget.

On a personal note I felt very proud in Dundalk when I commented on the large turn out. I said "It really shows you love our Club as much as we love your Country" and I received a brilliant reception, and I imagined my father standing behind me saying "Good on ye son!"

To the question, would I do it all again? I have no regrets as there is nothing I wouldn't do for Celtic. It is however a hypothetical question as the same circumstances could never happen again. The Club now belongs to the people. In the end this great feeling of pride will keep me warm in the coldest of winters; the pride that comes from knowing that I played my part in the rebirth of our Club. The only thing I want in return is a successful Celtic Football Club, back in its rightful place with the cream of Europe. That will have made all of this worthwhile.

There was a final twist of irony, the first game immediately after the takeover was at Perth where it all began, and, like all good stories, there was a happy ending as we won 1-0.'

Well, what can you say about that guy. I mean how could you possibly lose a campaign with the feeling and commitment Brendan just displayed there? When I described him earlier as a man born with green and white hoops on his heart I thought that would be the ultimate accolade for a Celtic supporter. But he is something else, born to be a Celt, a great man to have on your side. God bless him.

JOHN THOMPSON

My lifetime affection and involvement with Celtic is probably down to me being a product of the hoops graduation system. My family was typical of many who were traditionally connected with the East End of Glasgow. First and second generation Irish and a great uncle who once played a couple of games for the Club somewhere in the distant past.

As a toddler 40 odd years ago, my grandfather and uncle would take me to the games. Match days always seemed to be the same. I would be lifted over at the turnstiles, sat on a crash barrier, surrounded by noise and masses of men and boys, all urging the team on. From then on Saturday's games became part of my life. I was hooked.

As I grew older, my days as a schoolboy supporter, apart from the 7-1 cup final, were barren times. When the great Jock Stein arrived in the mid-1960s I had graduated to following the Bhoys from the 'Jungle'. The football I would witness during the next ten years set the standards for all my future aspirations for Celtic.

As time passed I got wiser, although my support for the team never waned. I advanced from the 'Jungle' to the 'Celtic End' and finally to the Main Stand, but on the park the team stood still. It was never quite able to raise itself to the dizzy heights of the Stein era. The stadium and the Club in general seemed to be in a time warp. Once feared and respected throughout Europe, Celtic had become ordinary. Passion, flair, and vision were all missing as we approached the 1988 Centenary year.

The three or four years prior had seen the departure of Billy McNeill, the embarrassing Rapid Vienna fiasco, the departures of good players and an influx of inferior ones and a league title won by literally falling over the line. The need for a new stadium was constant.

Our surveys show," according to then Chairman Jack McGinn, "that the vast majority of our support favour standing." It's taken ten years to rectify that peril of wisdom.

The date was January 1987. Provoked by new Chairman Jack McGinn's inaugural statement: "With the centenary year coming up I would like to see us win the European Cup again." I sat down and wrote a six-page letter to Tom Devlin (a Board member for 17 years) and who, as a supporter, I found approachable. My epistle suggested: "To win the European Cup the minimum entry qualification requires that you win the domestic league first." The contents secured me an audience at Celtic Park.

An hour and a half was spent covering the subjects that I raised. I pointed out that as things stood, Celtic were about to lose the services of McClair, McLeod, and Johnston by the end of the season. Tosh McKinlay is out of contract, so why didn't we sign him? What about letting the fans buy shares in the Club? A certain other stadium was light years ahead of ours: why not rebuild; improve the catering; put in executive boxes; install a sponsored electronic scoreboard; invest in the boys club; install a Celtic phone-in?

I vividly remember the answer concerning the phone-in. Quote: "We couldn't allow kids to run up expensive phone bills, their parents would go crazy." Our rivals installed one two weeks later, so did we.

As the parable says: "And some seed fell on stony ground."

The dye was cast. "A man who has to be convinced before he acts is not a man of action...You must act as you breathe." So wrote George Clemenceau.

I spent the next seven years campaigning in various ways. It had begun with letter-writing and the occasional phone-in. It progressed through my membership of the Supporters Association, the small shareholders and rebel group of investors and, ultimately, to my alliance with fellow supporters in 'Celts For Change'.

The takeover period has been well-documented. It changed my outlook and opinions on life. On the positive side, the time, effort and dedication and the finance that many Celtic-minded people put in, coupled with their great love for the Club, truly amazed me. Equally I found the deceit, abuse of power, privilege and greed I came across extremely distasteful.

I and Celtic FC should be eternally grateful to my wife and daughter. God knows how they put up with it all. Me out campaigning every night or so during those six months; coming home in those early hours of the morning; disrupting meal times; interfering with the family social life; never off the phone; no time to sit down and talk with them. The two of them acting as unpaid secretaries, drivers, signwriters etc. Without their understanding, love and backing, I doubt very much if I could have maintained the level of pressure on the Board during the run-in.

Make no mistake, the demands on your immediate family can affect their health as well as your own. Everyone ends up suffering from lack of sleep, poor eating habits and the unbelievable stress of it all. Everyone's work suffers. I was regularly travelling up and down to work on company business during the times the rallies were being held. Catching the 7.15am shuttle to London, back that evening, and off to a rally at 7.30pm. Home after midnight, two hours typing and faxing press releases. Rushing here, rushing there...it all finally catches up with you.

There are also financial implications for you and your family. Often they can be overlooked in the short term, at a later date they can be most damaging. There is no way a person can put equal effort into two entirely different tasks. One has to suffer.

Personally, I lost out on the guarantee of 18 months continuous work-security for my family. I would not even venture a guess at the cost of lost business, the cost of phone calls, faxes, petrol and countless other overheads that I incurred. You have to put the experience behind you. These days there are few, if any, willing to show concern outside their own family.

"Would I do it again?" I doubt it! It has taken a sizeable chunk of my family's life. I met with some wonderful people and true supporters. People I can truthfully call friends. Those with whom I could stand up and be counted. Even during such a serious time there were many humorous, kind and eventful things to remember. Unfortunately, on the negative side, there were those who at best could be described as hypocrites, liars and only interested in their own self interests. Nowadays I think I am a bit old for the role of front-line activist and there are many others, younger and equally as passionate. I'm sure they would do a better job. But for the right reasons I'd always be willing to give advice, especially where the Celtic were concerned.

Another, at times, harrowing account of personal sacrifice. A man's employment affected, and disruption to his family's health and home life. If there was a price for such commitment, where would you start? Another man who stood up for what was right.

I have now asked the question of all the lads involved, so I suppose it is my turn to answer the question. Would I do it all again? I have often asked myself this before now. I don't think you can go through life losing and jeopardising loves and personal relationships. As a Sunday dad I can still hear the sounds of disappointment in my children's voices when I phoned to cancel an arrangement once again. That's not fair, and you can't live your life like that.

I also recall coming home at night, after speaking to 1600 or so people and sitting in my house alone because the campaign had wrecked something and someone I could possibly have spent a good part of my life with. I also went through a period of having to borrow money for necessary household costs which rose inexorably.

These examples are costs, and like most things in life, you end up counting the cost. My Mother at 70 was a pillar of support and a good listener when reptiles attempted to smear my character. Could I ask the same of her again at her age? Celtic are a wonderful love to us all but we have to survive in life and be practical about what is going on around about us. Our responsibilities in life are our families, our work, our loves. At the end of the day these are the most important things and they must be protected. I know, I've been there.

These are the views of the men who all contributed in their own small way. They came from nowhere and they went back to nowhere. I remember former Celtic reserve Andy Ritchie saying at the end of the campaign on Q96 Radio: "Matt McGlone should go back to where he came from." I did, and thanks for your kind thoughts and sentiments Andy. I went back to where I came from and you were then given a coaching job at Celtic Park thanks to the change that took place.

Sharing the Club

At the end of November 1994 I went to Toronto for a week's holiday and stayed with my mate Davie and his wife Lisa. There is quite a large following of Celtic supporters in that part of Canada, most of them having emigrated in the early 1960s as the offers of work there were far more attractive than they were here at the time. Many of them have their own supporters clubs which are fully equipped with satellite systems which pick up the majority of games Celtic are involved in.

I went to visit the Bramalea CSC and ended up on the platform speaking to supporters about a whole host of things. What I discovered, that may have been overlooked by the Club, was the fact that these overseas Celts were really keen to buy shares.

Myself and David Low returned in January 1995 and toured several clubs who wanted to get in on the action. We returned to Bramalea and a healthy crowd attended, purchasing tens of thousands of dollars worth of shares. Other clubs also attended this venue amongst them the Durham CSC and the London CSC.

We also visited the Scarboro CSC who have their own club fully equipped with the important things like, well, a bar for a start! Again a healthy turnout guaranteed thousands of dollars worth of Celtic shares purchased.

In the struggle for the Celtic soul many people played major roles and very often they didn't get much of a mention. Jim Doherty is one of these people. In a world where people grab what they can Jim found himself the guardian and owner of 860 Celtic shares. These original Celtic shares could easily have been purchased for £300.00 a time at the height of the battle for Celtic. Jim Doherty refused to sell these shares for that price in order to help achieve change. This man, who has a wife and a family to look after, was not big on football but was big on principle.

To give you a rough idea of his steadfastness, imagine you had £258,000 worth of shares in the Toronto Blue Jays and you lived in Glasgow, and a takeover was going on at the Blue Jays and you were offered £300.00 per share knowing that in a few months they would only be worth, say, £70.00. Be honest, what would you do? Jim did what he thought was right. He kept the shares on the side of the rebels and refused the Kelly shilling. Another who stood up to be counted.

From Scarboro CSC we headed down to St Catharines near Niagara Falls, not that we could visit them as the Canadian winter had set in and that 8 mile trip was impossible. This meeting took in the above club along with the Jock Stein Memorial CSC from Hamilton, Ontario, and the Burlington CSC also from Ontario. Apart from the share sale, question and answer sessions were also held.

From there it was up to Montreal CSC. Now this was a bit different to say the least. This sales meeting was to be held in a Greek restaurant as other diners munched away.

Myself and David were picked up and brought to this eating house on the outskirts of the city. Now these meetings are not just a matter of turning up and asking people to give you a cheque before filling in a form. A sales pitch on why you should buy shares in our Club is required, and that takes at least a couple of hours. I talked on the meaning of being a supporter and what this Club means to us all. David covered the business side of the issue.

I have spoken in many precarious and unusual situations but never over the top of people who are out having a meal, and who are not part of the Celtic evening. We eventually moved the show into the bar, with a neon Budweiser sign shining above my head.

Talk of the takeover came up and one fan in particular, who was giving David a really hard time, started on me and asked why we campaigned against Sir Bob Kelly because he was a good guy. I attempted to explain that Bob Kelly had been dead for a number of years and perhaps if he had been around things may not have got to the stage they did, but to no avail. I'm afraid there was no telling this guy who was alive and who wasn't!

The Ottawa CSC were also in attendance and they purchased a few shares along with the Montreal boys. Now to save this chap's embarrassment I won't name him, but he picked us up from the hotel in downtown Montreal and we assumed that we were getting a return trip. But at the end of the evening, and after he had sunk a few bottles of his favourite juice, he informs Mr Low and myself that he is for the off and that it was nice meeting us. "Aren't you running us back to the hotel?" I enquired. "No sorry, I've had too much to drink," says he. Now this is like dropping a Canadian in the middle of Harthill and saying "Bye, bye". David pipes up: "Do you mind telling us where we are then?" This he does, and off he goes.

As he went we both stuck our heads out the door to watch him skidding all over the snow covered road in his car!

The overall total raised from the sale of shares during our visits to these Celtic clubs was a staggering 250,000 dollars!

The completed forms had cheques written out in Canadian dollars and had to be changed into sterling and delivered to the bank in Edinburgh before noon the following day. We flew the economical route via Amsterdam. Because of the shares deadline we both sat up the entire night on the flight over the Atlantic sorting out the currency change and paperwork. By the time we arrived in Amsterdam at 6.45am the work still hadn't been completed. As we worked away furiously with all this Celtic paperwork spread out on the Schipol Airport floor travellers were dodging by in an attempt not to stand on the share forms. By the time we arrived in Glasgow the Edinburgh deadline was only two hours away.

As we walked through customs, I said to David: "I'll bet we get stopped here."

"Hey, can we have a look in your bags sir?"

As the customs man went through our stuff he asked if we had a nice time in Canada. I asked how he knew we were in Canada.

Remember we had just come off a flight from Amsterdam. He replied that he had watched us both fly out the previous week. Interesting. Did you ever read George Orwell's book 1984?

As he opened my last bag the old West of Scotland attitude reared it's head, and we had only been back in the country a matter of minutes. He picked my Celtic scarf out from the top of my holdall and held it up to his mate before shouting: "Hey look at this. Is this not a good enough reason to give his bag a search?" Some things never change!

Foundations and the Future

From the vulture's perch, where our Club is so often viewed from, we can now see new horizons. We have a ground being redeveloped to the standards required for the customer in the 21st century.

We have a proper business structure in position. We have a new management team in place at a cost and a manager who is just like you or I in that he cares about the Club and its principles. Now you may think that's a touch parochial, and perhaps it is. But for better or worse that is the situation we created and it is the environment we operate in.

And that is where we differ from any other team. The closest comparable club is possibly Liverpool who, like ourselves, promote from within. The reason for this is that to function in our world you must understand the hopes and expectations of the Club's followers; you must know the nature of the beast.

We varied from that path just once in our history and appointed Liam Brady as manager. My opinion of Brady was that if he didn't understand the expectations then he would soon learn, possibly the hard way. I interviewed Brady once and as I sat opposite him in the manager's office I sensed he was perhaps struggling to come to terms with what he was in charge of.

That's not a criticism of Liam. It's an appraisal of the situation. My fears regarding Liam's freshness to our culture were highlighted in this question and answer session.

Q. Does the Celtic fans' enthusiasm for the Club surprise you?

A. Yes I would have to say it's almost beyond football.

And it is, and that is exactly what creates the extra pressure if you don't understand it. 99% of teams on this island are football teams. We are a football team and a culture. Now to manage both at one time is a pretty awesome task. But that is what a Celtic manager is taking on. I then asked Liam:

Q. What do you think are the main differences between Scottish and English football?

A. There is more competition in England. I would really like to get Celtic included in that kind of league, simply because it is not nice to be expected to win every game. I think the attitude of our supporters would change if we played in that type of league.

Well, would it? Is it because of our intense dislike of Rangers? They, after all, are the very opposite to our type of culture. Is that the reason we cannot take a breather from possible success, because if we do that, then they will win what we don't?

Regarding what Brady said about playing in England. It would then mean that we wouldn't apply so much intense pressure to our own Club simply because it wouldn't always be Rangers winning what we failed to win, there would be others.

Is what we love, and the demands that makes, too much for Celtic managers to operate under? I think not, although it is a very difficult working environment. It is also a very unique situation, in as much as what is achieved by managing a successful Celtic side is surely the pinnacle of any Celtic man's life.

These very pressures hung over Tommy Burns like a vengeful mother in law in the 1995 Scottish Cup Final. The absolute need to win was heightened further by our disastrous defeat in the Coca-Cola Final and the six barren years we experienced prior to that.

There were plenty of reasons for this barren spell but they were all deposited on Tommy Burns and that's quite a burden to work under. It all comes back to our expectations and needs.

Our needs off the park are now being handled in a more businesslike manner. I had an inkling of what required immediate attention at our Club when it changed ownership. People may never realise the mess it was left in and the cleaning up that took place. On many an occasion when a filing cabinet was pulled open you wouldn't really know what to expect to see inside.

Yet there have been constant knockers from day one of the takeover.

People of a weaker nature may have taken six months of all that hassle and then said "I've had enough of this. I came here to help you and you constantly knock everything I attempting to achieve. Goodbye."

And then what would have happened? All the talkers would have been flushed out into the open, but could they or would they have done any better? That for me has been the most disappointing aspect of the takeover. People coming in to help and taking a major financial risk and being criticised for looking the wrong way. Every single person who put money into our Club from the top to the bottom took one major risk with their cash.

The trouble with a club like Celtic is everybody wants a piece of the action. Celtic are a powerful force on a psychological level and are also a powerful force within the day to day running of people's lives. If you have a little bit of the Celtic action you will be reluctant to ever give it up. That is the very reason people started to flap when faced with the notion that change may be on the cards. From the Board downwards a great deal of people thought only of how it would affect their own little part of the gravy train.

These people though who thought that this was of paramount importance are damaging the very Club they claim to love. The attitude of "What's in it for me mate," will only eat away at the very foundation of Celtic.

If we can love Celtic for what they are, and what they represent, rather than what we can make from them, we will always get the best from them. The Club does not exist to be exploited. It's there to be enjoyed. Celtic are a vehicle for our identity and if we throw our arms around it and protect it, it will still be there for our children. If we don't protect it what is there left?

Hail Hail!